NEW JERUSALEM CITY OF GOD
INTERNATIONAL

Are You *Really* Saved?

Common Christian Fables About Salvation

Karen McNeil

JOSHUA GENERATION PRESS
Sausalito, CA

Published by Joshua Generation Press
3001 Bridgeway Blvd., Suite 250
Sausalito, CA 94965

ISBN: 978-0-9903132-0-5

DEDICATION

This book is dedicated in loving memory to my mother and dear friend, Miriam Arie Trotter McNeil.

It is also dedicated to my children, Kyle and Joy. Thank you for faithfully traveling this long journey with me in the arduous pursuit of truth.

CONTENTS

AN OPEN DOOR vii

Introduction. ix

PART 1 1

Sheep and Goats *1*

1   That Burning Question 3

2   The Lost Book. 9

3   The Benefits Of Kingdom Citizenship. 17

PART 2 21

God's True Plan Of Salvation *21*

4   Simple Math 23

Repentance *25*

5   Repentance Fables. 27

6   Journey Of A King's Heart 35

Water Baptism In The Name Of Jesus Christ *41*

7   Water Baptism Fables 43

Baptism Of The Spirit *67*

8   The Adoption Process 69

9   Baptism Of The Spirit Fables 75

10   The Baptism Experience 107

Faith *117*

11   Faith Fables 119

12   The Ultimate Faith Fable 141

PART 3 . . . . **153**

Wise Choices *153*

13   Choose Truth 155

14   Choose Holiness 159

15   Choose Salvation 163

PART 4 . . . . **165**

One Lost Sheep *165*

16   The Final Appointment 167

17   The Faith To Move A Mountain 169

18   A Miraculous Healing 175

19   A Long Journey Home 183

20   Miriam's Song 193

Author's Note 199

HOW TO CONNECT WITH OUR COMMUNITY **201**

The Desperate Zone 203

AN OPEN DOOR

And to the angel of the church in Philadelphia write; These things saith he that is holy, he that is true, he that hath the key of David, he that openeth, and no man shutteth; and shutteth, and no man openeth;

I know thy works: behold, I have set before thee an open door, and no man can shut it: for thou hast a little strength, and hast kept my word, and hast not denied my name.

Behold, I will make them of the synagogue of Satan, which say they are Jews, and are not, but do lie; behold, I will make them to come and worship before thy feet, and to know that I have loved thee.

Because thou hast kept the word of my patience, I also will keep thee from the hour of temptation, which shall come upon all the world, to try them that dwell upon the earth.

Behold, I come quickly: hold that fast which thou hast, that no man take thy crown.

Him that overcometh will I make a pillar in the temple of my God, and he shall go no more out: and I will write upon him the name of my God, and the name of the city of my God, which is new Jerusalem, which cometh down out of heaven from my God: and I will write upon him my new name.

He that hath an ear, let him hear what the Spirit saith unto the churches.

—Revelation 3:7-13

Introduction

My passion for writing, teaching, and preaching about the importance of restoring biblical truth to the Church began in a deeply personal way through a painful journey that ultimately led to my salvation. It is a journey that saved my life and profoundly changed the lives of my children for the better, though for many years they certainly would have disagreed.

Together, we struggled through many grueling trials, often wondering if they ever would end. The challenges of life often seemed insurmountable. Nearly every aspect of our lives was disrupted and uprooted in one way or another, and nearly everything we faced seemed to require a miracle. Yet, through every trial, God moved mightily and often miraculously, preserving us in ways that defied all odds.

The true turning point in our journey came when I learned the truth about salvation and how to tap into the power of God. Initially, the miracles that occurred caught me completely by surprise. However, soon thereafter, I discovered that by applying the simple biblical principles you will read in this book, I was able to consistently experience the miracles of God.

Practical application of biblical truth enabled me to prevail over obstacles that should have destroyed my life. Over many years of rebuilding my own broken life, however, God taught me to live a life of miracles. He carefully navigated me around every obstacle, and He moved heaven and earth to ensure that I remained standing so I could preserve the lives of my children when they were most vulnerable.

As I neared the end of my journey, God finally said it was time for me to speak. He led me to establish an online community for women and He gave me the assignment to write this book. I want to share my story so you will understand why this book about salvation is really a book about collectively taking the first step toward saving our children.

The journey I have described began many years ago when I was at one of the lowest points in my life. I was a single mother with two young children who desperately needed me, yet, I, too, was in desperate need of help. It seemed as if I simply could not go on. Alone in my bedroom one day, I realized that I was sinking further and further into the depths of despair. Instead of fighting to live, I wanted to crawl into a small, dark place where I could just hide from life and die. Dying, however, was not an option. I was determined that even if I could not find a reason to live for myself, I had to find a way to live for my children.

My journey began many years ago when I was at one of the lowest points in my life. I was a single mother with two young children who desperately needed me, yet, I, too, was in desperate need of help. It seemed as if I simply could not go on. Alone in my bedroom one day, I realized that I was sinking further and further into the depths of despair. Instead of fighting to live, I wanted to crawl into a small, dark place where I could just hide from life and die. Dying, however, was not an option. I was determined that even if I could not find a reason to live for myself, I had to find a way to live for my children.

That day, in my brokenness, I found the help I needed in a gentle whisper from God. What He said to me initially sounded quite peculiar, but that one whisper from God gave me the faint ray of hope I needed to help me hold onto life. God began to speak to me that day about a tiny closet in my home. He told me to clean out that closet and make it a prayer closet. He said that whenever I needed to retreat to a safe, quiet place, I could go into my prayer closet to shut out the cares of the world. He promised that if I would enter into my closet to pray, He would meet me there, speak to my heart, and comfort me. So, that day, I obeyed the instructions God whispered into my heart.

I cleaned out the storage closet and converted it to a place of prayer. I went there daily, desperately searching for God. Sometimes I would kneel quietly and pray. Other times I would cry out to Him, pouring out the deepest hurts of my heart and soul. Often I would simply sit quietly, listening for hours, hoping to hear His small, still voice speak to me. Sometimes I waited so long that I would fall asleep in my little room.

The awkwardness of sitting alone in a prayer closet was initially difficult for me. Sometimes God said nothing at all. Sometimes He gave me simple instructions. Sometimes He spoke at length. In time, I discovered that my prayer closet was no longer an awkward, lonely place, but rather the only place where I consistently found peace and tranquility.

Eventually, I furnished that little room with some of my most cherished belongings and made it a second home within my home. Over many years, it evolved from a cluttered storage closet to a sterile, empty prayer closet, to my treasured sanctuary pictured on the cover of this book.

In my prayer closet, I learned to be completely intimate with God. I learned to surrender to His will. Most importantly, I learned to hear, believe, and obey Him. I am so thankful that God did not leave me alone to die in a dark, quiet place. Instead, He gently led me into a safe haven where He kept me for much longer than I ever could have imagined. Over a period of more than a decade, God healed my heart. He gave me the hope, courage, and determination to live. He taught me many spiritual lessons and practical life lessons. Yet, still, after all those years, I was empty. Something was missing.

I had spent nearly thirty years establishing a career that I once enjoyed. For many years, I worked with senior executives across a broad range of sectors, building leadership and organizational capability. My passion for that work, however, was long gone. My true passion was God and ministry and, in my mind, my career in business had no clear ties to a future in ministry. I simply could not understand why God had given me such a burning passion for building His kingdom without giving me a clear vision of how He intended to use me. Finally, He began to give me clarity about my life and my future work.

God began speaking to me about shifting my focus from building leadership capability in other organizations to building leadership and organizational capability in His kingdom. Still, His vision was not clear to me, so I tucked myself away in my prayer closet and fervently sought Him for greater clarity and direction.

Finally, early one summer God said there was something in particular that He wanted to show me. I sensed that I was finally getting close to His answer about my life's purpose. For nearly three months, He led me through a painstaking study of Bible basics about salvation. I knew there was something of great significance that He wanted me to see, but I couldn't quite put my finger on it. I was studying things that I was certain I had clearly understood for many years. Quite frankly, the study was so elementary and tedious that I was nearly bored to tears. Nonetheless, I diligently searched the Bible determined to find this big thing that God assured me I would soon discover. Then it hit me. When I finally found it, I was stunned.

Fables? Christian fables form the foundation of our beliefs about *salvation*?

All I could think is, "God, You expect me to believe that week after week, *in church*, we are learning fables about the biblical requirements for salvation? People all over the world have believed these fables? They think they're born again believers and in the kingdom of God when, in fact, they're not – and they don't know it? *That* absolutely cannot be true."

Well, sadly, it is quite true and therein lies the problem.

That summer, God gave me a deep revelation about foundational teachings on salvation that I had missed for years. By the end of the summer, I finally understood the gravity of the problem among Christians today. What I still didn't understand, however, is what, exactly, God wanted me to do with the rest of my life. Finally, one day near the end of that year, He answered my question with one word.

Children.

At first, I didn't understand. Then something happened. In that moment, I felt as if God placed His heart inside me so I could feel what He feels. I will never forget the depth of emotion I experienced that day. I was distraught as I felt the anguish, grief, and gut wrenching pain in God's heart. It is the grief that daily pierces His soul as He examines the shattered lives of our children. As a mother whose children are my treasure, I finally understood. I wept bitterly as God spoke to me that day about the condition of the lives of our children.

Look around. How recently have you examined the plight of the precious children in your own backyard and those around the world? The problem is painfully obvious. Every single day, children, youth, and young adults all over the world are being savagely destroyed.

Some are self-destructing because they are seeking answers to their problems in all the wrong places. Some are being destroyed by other young people who have lost their way, their sense of humanity, and often their minds. Many are being destroyed by negligent and predatory adults, including their own parents, who have also lost their way in life.

What is happening to our children is not a mystery. They are being destroyed because *we* have missed the absolute simplicity of salvation. It is time for change. It is time for change in our lives. It is long past time for change in our children's lives.

Our children are our future. God entrusted them to us to love, protect, and equip so they will be well able to lead and advance His kingdom. Psalm 127:3-6 says:

> *Lo, children are an heritage of the Lord: and the fruit of the womb is his reward. As arrows are in the hand of a mighty man; so are children of the youth. Happy is the man that hath his quiver full of them: they shall not be ashamed, but they shall speak with the enemies in the gate.*

This world is full of beautiful children who come in all shapes, sizes and colors. Each has a unique personality. Each has a unique destiny to fulfill. God created them to be mighty arrows in His quiver. Yet, all over the world so many of our precious children have become broken arrows.

Far too many of them are silently struggling with their own shattered lives, often wrestling with problems created by unresolved issues in their parents' lives. Many are fighting to heal from life experiences that are unspeakable. Our children are desperately searching for meaning in the midst of a world increasingly characterized by absolute madness. Life for many of them is rapidly unraveling. Yet, sooner than we think, these broken young people will be the parents and leaders who will set the course of destiny for generations to come.

Our children need healing. They need it so they can experience the joy that Jesus Christ came to give them. They need it so they can become the next generation of leaders in the kingdom of God and in the world. If we fail to address the issues of their lives today, they will be ill-equipped to address the considerable leadership challenges they will soon face in every area of life.

Family. Religion. Education. Business. Government. Arts & Entertainment. Media. These societal pillars form the infrastructure of our lives. One day soon, today's young people will rule it all. Many things about the future are uncertain. However, we can be certain of this - it is in *no one's* best interest to place power and control of the global infrastructure of our planet in the hands of young people who do not know Jesus. We must equip our children with a solid, Christ-centered foundation. We must develop them for the leadership challenges that lie ahead or the lives of the children who come after them will be destined for destruction.

Reclaiming our children begins with us individually and collectively returning to God's original plan given to us in Genesis 1:28. It says:

> *And God blessed them, and God said unto them, Be fruitful, and multiply, and replenish the earth, and subdue it: and have dominion over the fish of the sea, and over the fowl of the air, and over every living thing that moveth upon the earth.*

Be fruitful. Multiply. Replenish the earth. Subdue it. Have dominion. That was the original plan. It hasn't changed, nor has God's clear directive for us to execute it.

What changed is that we lost the competitive advantage that enables us to execute the plan with ease when Adam and Eve got thrown out of the garden of Eden. Thankfully, we regained our advantage when Jesus Christ extended to us the opportunity to secure our salvation. Without salvation, we have neither the power nor the authority to have dominion over anything. With salvation, we have the power and authority to have dominion over everything.

That is why on Pentecost, the day that marks the beginning of the Church, Peter preached a powerful sermon that ends with an open invitation to salvation. Acts 2:39 tells us that in his sermon, Peter spoke of God's promise that is for us *and* for our children. Why? Because the problems we and our children experience can be overwhelming and complex, but the answer is not. In one way or another, salvation is the simple answer to every problem we will ever face. More importantly, it establishes where we and our children will spend eternity.

I confess that initially it wasn't apparent to me what my study of salvation that summer had to do with children, nor was it clear how my prior work experience in leadership development fit into God's plan. However, as I neared the end of that long, painful journey, God began to connect the dots of my life. After over a decade of being quietly tucked away in my prayer closet, fasting, praying, and listening to God, I finally had the answer to the question of my life's purpose.

Children. Salvation. Leadership development. Dominion.

So, how did this book find its way into your hands? Perhaps you're reading it out of curiosity. Perhaps you're reading it because your life is like mine was when I first cleaned out that tiny closet. Desperately in need of healing for all the broken places in your life. Desperately in need of help with your children. Desperately in need of answers from God. Desperately in need of change. Through it all, you have held onto the hope that just maybe God is still the God of miracles. Perhaps your prayer today is that He will become the God of miracles *for you.* I encourage you to trust and believe with your whole heart that every blessing and every miracle you need is waiting for you in the kingdom of God. This book is the map that will lead you there.

Today I invite you to find the truth in the pages of this book. Practical application of biblical truth will enable you to step boldly through the open door Jesus speaks of in Revelation 3:8.

Listen closely as the Word of God speaks to you. One tiny whisper from Jesus can and will change the trajectory of your life. Now, quiet your spirit and listen for those gentle whispers as the King of glory speaks into your heart and leads you to the place where He awaits you.

PART 1

Sheep and Goats

And he shall set the sheep on his right hand, but the goats on the left.

—*Matthew 25:33*

CHAPTER 1

That Burning Question

Look around and you will see many faces. Perhaps you will be tempted to classify them into groups. Young. Old. Rich. Poor. Black. White. Men. Women. Resist the temptation. The simple truth is that there are only two groups that matter to God. They should be the only two groups that matter to us.

The Bible calls them sheep and goats. Sheep are those who will hear, believe, and obey God. Goats are those who will desperately wish they had. The ultimate dividing line between the two is found in the answer to that burning question Jesus is asking each of us.

Are you *really* saved?

It is a simple question, yet our answer charts the course of destiny in this life and into eternity. That is why it is imperative that we make it our highest priority to get the right answer now while there is still time.

Unfortunately, the standard answer offered by most who profess to be Christians is an emphatic, "Of course, I'm saved!" It is that universal sense of certainty about our salvation that brings us face to face with the central problem in the Church today.

It is not our belief that we are saved that secures our salvation. It is the inerrant Word of God that determines whether or not we are saved. Until we do what the Bible instructs us to do to establish our salvation, we cannot rightfully claim that we are saved.

Increasingly, as more Christians begin to carefully examine God's Word for themselves, many will soon come to a difficult conclusion. They will discover that they have not fully met the biblical requirements to establish their salvation.

Does that mean that God does not love them or that He has somehow rejected them? It does not. He loves them enough to have sent His only begotten Son to die for them. Does it mean that they do not love God? It does not. Many people who love God and faithfully serve Him to the best of their ability simply have not yet heard the full truth. Without hearing it, they cannot believe or obey it. I am the first to admit that I was shocked when I learned that I was one of those people.

I deeply loved God, attended church regularly, and routinely read and studied the Bible. I was active in ministry, teaching what I knew to others, including my children. Serving God to the best of my ability was of utmost importance to me and I put forth my best effort. Since I had done all that I had been taught, of course, I was absolutely certain of my salvation.

Then, through a series of miracles, God strategically connected me to key people He handpicked to place in my life. Those individuals taught and preached the uncompromising truth of God's Word. They tutored me and, in time, God used them to lead me into a deeper understanding of many biblical truths.

It was through those experiences that I first made the disturbing discovery that, according to God's Word, I had only recently secured my salvation. I simply did not want to believe that I wasn't *really* saved all those years that I thought I was, so I faced a sobering dilemma. God and I had a difference of opinion about my salvation and I had to decide whose opinion I would ultimately believe.

Fortunately, I was well acquainted with God's position concerning my dilemma. When we encounter two different opinions about anything and one of those opinions belongs to God, the other opinion is always unquestionably wrong.

I had to accept that God was right. I unknowingly had been walking in ignorance about my salvation for years. That jolting encounter with truth shook me to the core of my soul. I struggled to reconcile the great contradictions between His Word and the teachings and beliefs that had become so deeply rooted in my heart.

As God led me through the painful process of reexamining my own religious beliefs, I suddenly recognized a much bigger and deeply troubling issue. These Christian fables about salvation that I had learned in church form the doctrinal foundation of what is commonly preached and taught in churches all around the world. That was terribly difficult for me to accept. I could have accepted that we cannot all be experts in all areas. There are many deep theological topics of study that most of us, including many pastors, may never understand.

But salvation?

That was a disruptive, almost unfathomable revelation that nearly shattered the foundations of my faith. That summer, as I studied the Bible, I often vacillated between belief and unbelief. At times I felt personally violated and offended by the knowledge that my once strong beliefs about salvation were wrong. Sometimes I wanted to shut out the truth and return to my old beliefs for my own peace of mind. I *needed* them to be true. Other times, when I was willing to acknowledge the truth, I felt angry that it had taken so long for me to discover it.

Finally, I had to make a decision. I had to choose once and for all whether to believe God or not. I knew that I did not have to believe God; I only had to believe Him if I wanted my salvation.

Ultimately, I chose to shift my focus to what was most important. Instead of focusing on having to release old beliefs, I focused on being grateful for what God had done for me. God loved me enough to take me by the hand and lead me into truth so that I could be saved if I was willing to hear, believe, and obey His Word.

I finally embraced what I had learned and allowed that disruptive experience with truth to lead me into a more careful examination of the Word of God. I became determined to find the whole truth about God's plan of salvation.

In the end, my personal encounter with those disruptive truths about salvation convinced me of one thing: I am *not* alone. Many people who believe they are saved will read this book and discover that they, too, are in the same situation.

Perhaps you're wondering how it is possible that so many people who feel absolutely assured of their salvation could be so wrong. That was certainly a question that I, too, asked of God. The answer is simple.

If we have not been properly taught what the Word of God says about salvation, it is highly improbable that we will do what is required. How, then, is it possible that so many people who sit in church every week have not been taught the biblical requirements for salvation? That, too, is quite simple.

All around us, Christian fables about salvation are being taught under the label of sound biblical doctrine. For generations, fables have been taught in our homes, in prominent seminaries, and in churches all around the world. Small country churches, urban mega churches, black churches, white churches, multi-cultural churches, rich churches, and poor churches. Every hour of every day, fables about salvation are broadcast globally on television, radio, and over the Internet.

Unfortunately, we do not recognize these teachings as fables because of their pervasiveness. We believe them because we listen to them week after week without carefully examining them against the Word of God. Consequently, they have become so deeply entrenched and tightly woven into the fabric of our churches and our society that we accept them as biblical truths. The result is that people have hung their hopes, lives, and souls on fables instead of the true plan of salvation that is clearly written in God's Word.

That truth should not come as a surprise to us. The Bible clearly warns us in 2 Timothy 4:2-4 that we will turn to fables. It says:

> *Preach the word; be instant in season, out of season; reprove, rebuke, exhort with all long suffering and doctrine.*

> *For the time will come when they will not endure sound doctrine; but after their own lusts shall they heap to themselves teachers, having itching ears;*

And they shall turn away their ears from the truth, and shall be turned unto fables.

We are no longer waiting for that time to come as this passage cautions us. Without question, the time has arrived. From seminaries, to pulpits, to church pews, many have strayed far from biblical truth, replacing God's Word with Christian fables. Consequently, a staggering number of people who love God are experiencing dire consequences in their lives without understanding why.

That is why God is speaking to us in this hour with such great clarity and urgency. He is sounding a blaring alarm about the importance of securing our salvation in accordance with the doctrine outlined in His Word.

Let us be clear. The Son of man will surely return. When He arrives there are only two possible outcomes for each of us. We will be counted among the sheep or we will be counted among the goats. Matthew 25:31-34 tells us what will happen to the sheep. It says:

When the Son of man shall come in his glory, and all the holy angels with him, then shall he sit upon the throne of his glory:

And before him shall be gathered all nations: and he shall separate them one from another, as a shepherd divideth his sheep from the goats:

And he shall set the sheep on his right hand, but the goats on the left.

Then shall the King say unto them on his right hand, Come, ye blessed of my Father, inherit the kingdom prepared for you from the foundation of the world:

This is what Matthew 25: 41 tells us about the fate of goats:

Then shall he say also unto them on the left hand, Depart from me, ye cursed, into everlasting fire, prepared for the devil and his angels:

There is no complexity. It's very simple. Sheep go to heaven. Goats go to the lake of fire. There is no third choice.

So, the burning question that Jesus is challenging each of us to answer in this hour is not, "Do you profess to be saved?" It is not, "Did your professor, pastor, priest, mother, father, sister, brother, husband, wife, or friends tell you that you are saved?" It is not, "Do you hope, feel, and believe that you're saved?"

The burning question is, "Are you *really* saved?" I strongly encourage you to wait until you have finished reading this book before answering the question.

CHAPTER 2

The Lost Book

Jesus Christ began His ministry with a simple message recorded in Mark 1:14-15. It says:

> . . . *Jesus came into Galilee, preaching the gospel of the kingdom of God,*
>
> *And saying, The time is fulfilled, and the kingdom of God is at hand: repent ye, and believe the gospel.*

This timeless message of repentance and belief in the Gospel must become the foundation of the life of every Christian. But what happens when we discover that the gospel we have heard and believed is not the Gospel that Jesus and His apostles taught and preached?

When we encounter biblical truth that is radically different than what we have come to believe, rather than repenting and believing the Gospel, we often reject the truth and return to our fables. That is why this chapter is devoted to a careful examination of three Bible stories. They are the stories

God led me to study as I struggled with the process of repenting for believing false doctrine and learning to believe the Gospel.

The first two stories helped me accept what Ecclesiastes 1:9 tells us. There is nothing new under the sun. History simply repeats itself, even in the house of God. The third story gave me great hope that I, too, could live a life of miracles if I would open my heart enough to hear, believe, and obey the Gospel.

The first story found in 2 Kings 22 and 23 records an almost unbelievable situation faced by religious leaders and their followers. I encourage you to carefully read both chapters on your own, but let's explore 2 Kings 22:3-13 together to see how the story begins:

> *And it came to pass in the eighteenth year of king Josiah, that the king sent Shaphan the son of Azaliah, the son of Meshullam, the scribe, to the house of the Lord, saying,*
>
> *Go up to Hilkiah the high priest, that he may sum the silver which is brought into the house of the Lord, which the keepers of the door have gathered of the people:*
>
> *And let them deliver it into the hand of the doers of the work, that have the oversight of the house of the Lord: and let them give it to the doers of the work which is in the house of the Lord, to repair the breaches of the house,*
>
> *Unto carpenters, and builders, and masons, and to buy timber and hewn stone to repair the house.*
>
> *Howbeit there was no reckoning made with them of the money that was delivered into their hand, because they dealt faithfully.*
>
> *And Hilkiah the high priest said unto Shaphan the scribe, I have found the book of the law in the house of the Lord. And Hilkiah gave the book to Shaphan, and he read it.*

And Shaphan the scribe came to the king, and brought the king word again, and said, Thy servants have gathered the money that was found in the house, and have delivered it into the hand of them that do the work, that have the oversight of the house of the Lord.

And Shaphan the scribe shewed the king, saying, Hilkiah the priest hath delivered me a book. And Shaphan read it before the king.

And it came to pass, when the king had heard the words of the book of the law, that he rent his clothes.

And the king commanded Hilkiah the priest, and Ahikam the son of Shaphan, and Achbor the son of Michaiah, and Shaphan the scribe, and Asahiah a servant of the king's, saying,

Go ye, enquire of the Lord for me, and for the people, and for all Judah, concerning the words of this book that is found: for great is the wrath of the Lord that is kindled against us, because our fathers have not hearkened unto the words of this book, to do according unto all that which is written concerning us.

Imagine that. The high priest stumbles upon the living Word of God that has been completely lost in God's house. Yet, all the while, the priests have continued to hold services, the people have continued to come, and the door keepers have continued to routinely collect money from them for maintenance of the facility.

The clear question is, "If the priests had no knowledge of the book of the law, what, exactly, were they teaching God's people?" There is no middle ground on the matter. They were either teaching doctrinal truth or they were teaching doctrinal fables. The painfully obvious answer is that they were teaching religious fables.

We later learn that the crisis is not resolved until the men return to the king with an answer from God spoken through the prophetess. When Josiah hears the message, he realizes there is only one solution to their considerable problems. The solution is *repentance*.

The king swiftly gathers all the people, including the priests and prophets, into the house of God and reads them the book of the law. He repents for their sins, then leads them in making a solemn oath to restore their broken covenant with God. Finally, he institutes sweeping reforms across the land to right the wrongs that have so deeply offended the Lord.

A second story that describes this "lost book" phenomenon is recorded in Nehemiah. In the opening chapter we find that God has allowed the vast majority of the Jews to be carried away into captivity. When Nehemiah, who serves in the palace in Shushan, inquires about the fate of the few Jews who manage to escape and remain in Jerusalem, he receives a sobering report.

The people are living in great affliction and reproach. The wall of their city is utterly destroyed and the gates of the city are burned with fire.

The root cause of their captivity and destruction is also found in the first chapter. After days of fasting and weeping, Nehemiah confesses in despondent prayer that he and the people, once again, have forsaken their covenant with God. The broken covenant is the reason God has led His people into captivity and allowed great destruction to fall upon those who are left behind.

Fortunately, God is deeply moved by Nehemiah's prayer. He allows Nehemiah to lead the people, in the face of great adversity, through the grueling work of rebuilding and restoring the infrastructure of their city. When the wall is rebuilt, the gates are repaired, and the people are safe again, they begin the next phase of their restoration.

Chapter 8 records the spiritual restoration that occurs when Ezra the priest, like Josiah, gathers all the people together in the streets and reads them the book of the law from morning until midday. When the people finally come to an understanding of the Word of God, they mourn and weep. Ezra, however, encourages their hearts. He instructs them not to mourn, but to be joyful in the Lord because the day is holy to God. He encourages them to celebrate their newly acquired understanding of God's unchanging Word.

The story, however, does not end with their celebration. The following chapter reveals what is required after the celebration. Chapter 9 records how the people are reminded of their considerable sins against God. They acknowledge that the great destruction and affliction in their lives is a direct result of their sin. They acknowledge God's patience and faithfulness toward them even in the face of their rebellion. Finally, Nehemiah 9:38 records the action the people are required to take. Once again, they must *repent* and "make a sure covenant" with God.

Truly, there is nothing new under the sun. The "lost book" among God's people is not a new phenomenon. Fables being taught in lieu of sound doctrine is not a new sin, destruction is not a new consequence, and repentance is not a new solution. God said that history repeats itself. Clearly, it is time for us to believe God.

Church as usual didn't work for the people in these stories and it isn't working for us. The answer to our individual and collective problems isn't more church as usual. We need an up-close and personal encounter with Jesus Christ that dramatically changes the circumstances of our lives. There is only one way to get it. If we want to see change in our lives and in the lives of our children, we must be open to making the changes God requires of us.

Changing deeply rooted religious beliefs certainly must have been difficult for the people in these two stories. It will be difficult for many of us. However, when we reach our tipping point, we *will* change. Our tipping point occurs when the pain of our present circumstances outweighs the pain of making the changes God requires of us so we can have a better future.

The final story I want to share is one of hope for miraculous new beginnings for those of us who are truly ready to experience lasting, positive change. The story, found in John 3, is about a man I believe may have reached his tipping point when the pain in his life compelled him to seek Jesus in a deeply personal way.

Nicodemus was a Pharisee, a prominent ruler of the Jews, and a man intimately connected to the establishment. By day, his allegiance was to the religious leaders who closely scrutinized Jesus, aggressively persecuted Him, and shamelessly discredited His ministry. Determined to protect their own interests, the Pharisees worked diligently to persuade their followers that Jesus was quite simply a fraud. Nicodemus clearly understood that as a Pharisee, he, too, was obligated to portray to the people that the religious status quo was working just fine – for him and for them. I believe, however, that what happened one particular night sheds a much different light on the issues of Nicodemus' life and what he truly believed. Let's examine the text.

John 3:1-5 says:

> *There was a man of the Pharisees, named Nicodemus, a ruler of the Jews:*
>
> *The same came to Jesus by night, and said unto him, Rabbi, we know that thou art a teacher come from God: for no man can do these miracles that thou doest, except God be with him.*
>
> *Jesus answered and said unto him, Verily, verily, I say unto thee, Except a man be born again, he cannot see the kingdom of God.*
>
> *Nicodemus saith unto him, How can a man be born when he is old? can he enter the second time into his mother's womb, and be born?*
>
> *Jesus answered, Verily, verily, I say unto thee, Except a man be born of water and of the Spirit, he cannot enter into the kingdom of God.*

So why would a Pharisee and leader of the religious sect that feared and hated Jesus arrange for a secret meeting with Him at night? The text tells us exactly what was on his mind. Nicodemus wanted to know about miracles. Why?

Perhaps Nicodemus, like many of us, found himself alone that night deeply troubled by his own problems. Despite his outward appearance as a prominent religious leader, he finally had to admit a painful truth to himself. His religion just wasn't working. His eloquent religious rhetoric had failed him. His scholarly religious friends had no answers for him. His impressive religious attire that identified him as a man of great power, in fact, gave him no power at all.

Jesus, on the other hand, was getting quite different results in His ministry and Nicodemus knew it. The people who followed Jesus weren't experiencing religion as usual. Everywhere Jesus went, the power of God was dynamically transforming the lives of ordinary people through His miracles.

Everyone knew about the miracles. Just a few verses before we read about Nicodemus, John 2:23 tells us that many believed on Jesus' name because of the miracles He performed while in Jerusalem for the Passover. All the religious leaders were talking about them. In fact, Nicodemus acknowledged to Jesus that they knew He is a teacher sent from God because of the miracles He performed. So, despite what he and the other Pharisees may have said about Jesus publicly, privately Nicodemus had to confess that he desperately needed to know the secret to living a life of miracles.

When Nicodemus asked Jesus, He gave him the straight and simple answer. Miracles happen *in* the kingdom of God and there's only one way to get in. You must be born again. Yet, even when Jesus answered his question, Nicodemus didn't understand and Jesus had to explain it again.

Like Nicodemus, we, too, have heard that we must be born again. Yet, many of us, like Nicodemus, have misunderstood what it means because the Church has lost the book - again. The question is, "Will we learn from history?"

If we will open our hearts to the possibility that we have lost the truth, we can learn biblical principles from these stories that can transform our lives and the lives of our children. The first lesson is that even when our religion is broken, our God is not. Jesus Christ is still the King of glory and the God of great and mighty miracles. The kingdom of God is still the place where miracles happen. Being born again is still the only way to get in.

When we become born again believers who practically apply the living Word of God in our lives, we will find the healing, great miracles, and deliverance that we so desperately need and we will find the path to eternal life. For many of us, the journey will begin with hearing the true Gospel of Jesus Christ for the first time and establishing a brand new relationship with Him. For others, it will involve unlearning religious fables, embracing truth, and reestablishing our relationship with Jesus.

As you study the Bible for yourself through a careful examination of this book, I want to encourage you just as Ezra encouraged God's people. If you find yourself facing disruptive truths about your prior understanding of the Bible and what it means to be born again, don't be grieved.

Be encouraged and be thankful that God loves you enough to have opened your eyes. Be joyful in the Lord as God leads you into a closer relationship with Him through a deeper understanding of His Word. Celebrate your newly acquired understanding. Then, graciously accept our Savior's open invitation into His kingdom.

There is no shame or condemnation in repentance. Repentance is a precious gift from God. Simply repent. Believe the Gospel. Take the steps necessary to establish your "sure covenant" with Jesus Christ. Then watch Him heal your heart, restore the broken places in your life, and lead you into the abundant life He came to give you.

CHAPTER 3

The Benefits Of
Kingdom Citizenship

Many mistakenly believe that the time to reap the benefits of our salvation is when we die and go to heaven. The truth is that, as God's sheep, we begin enjoying the great benefits of salvation the moment we establish a covenant relationship with Him.

As soon as our salvation is established, our lives dramatically change regardless of whether we perceive the change. In that instant, we are ushered out of the kingdom of darkness and into the kingdom of God. God becomes our Father and our King and we become His children and citizens of His kingdom. We enter into a new level of intimacy with Him and He responds differently to our most urgent and routine needs.

As His children and citizens of His kingdom, God gives us access to His kingdom benefits plan. That plan is His covenant with us that is uniquely tailored to provide for the security and welfare of each citizen. Psalm 68:19-20 describes it in this way:

Blessed be the Lord, who daily loadeth us with benefits, even the God of our salvation. Selah.

He that is our God is the God of salvation; and unto GOD the Lord belong the issues from death.

Our salvation gives us a level of favor with God and man that often surpasses our comprehension. Daily, God loads our lives with the benefits of His salvation, giving us access to every kingdom blessing and deliverance from every adverse situation. When we are in the kingdom of God and in right standing with Him, we can rest securely in that precious promise.

Certainly, God extends a measure of His mercy and grace to everyone. Matthew 5:45 tells us that He makes His sun rise on the evil and on the good. He sends rain on the just and on the unjust. However, the covenant promises extended to the citizens of God's kingdom guarantee us a level of favor that we simply cannot afford to miss, particularly when trouble comes.

There are times in all of our lives when seemingly insurmountable challenges arise. When the storms of life surface, our covenant with God assures us that He will move heaven and earth on our behalf. He will deliver us from any and every peril up to and including death. He will do it because He is God and He cannot lie. He promised it and His Word cannot return to Him void. God's Word must accomplish its expressed purpose.

When the greatest trials of life surface, it may look as if there is no way out. However, when we are in right standing with God, we can trust and take comfort in the safety and security of Psalm 91. It says:

He that dwelleth in the secret place of the most High shall abide under the shadow of the Almighty.

I will say of the LORD, He is my refuge and my fortress: my God; in him will I trust.

Surely he shall deliver thee from the snare of the fowler, and from the noisome pestilence.

He shall cover thee with his feathers, and under his wings shalt thou trust: his truth shall be thy shield and buckler.

Thou shalt not be afraid for the terror by night; nor for the arrow that flieth by day;

Nor for the pestilence that walketh in darkness; nor for the destruction that wasteth at noonday.

A thousand shall fall at thy side, and ten thousand at thy right hand; but it shall not come nigh thee.

Only with thine eyes shalt thou behold and see the reward of the wicked.

Because thou hast made the LORD, which is my refuge, even the most High, thy habitation;

There shall no evil befall thee, neither shall any plague come nigh thy dwelling.

For he shall give his angels charge over thee, to keep thee in all thy ways.

They shall bear thee up in their hands, lest thou dash thy foot against a stone.

Thou shalt tread upon the lion and adder: the young lion and the dragon shalt thou trample under feet.

Because he hath set his love upon me, therefore will I deliver him: I will set him on high, because he hath known my name.

He shall call upon me, and I will answer him: I will be with him in trouble; I will deliver him, and honour him.

With long life will I satisfy him, and shew him my salvation.

Psalm 91 becomes deeply personal to us when God gives us firsthand experience of what it means to have Him navigate us safely through the most turbulent storms of life. Only then do we begin to understand the precious benefits of salvation and appreciate in a personal way what the seventh verse of Psalm 91 really means. That verse gives us a clear view of the battlefield when God is on our side. It promises us that a thousand will fall at our side and ten thousand will fall at our right hand, but destruction will not come near us.

Truly, there is nothing of greater value than our salvation. Family, friends, health, wealth, intellect, influence, beauty, and success are all nice to have. They certainly make life easier, but none come with guarantees. All of them can be stripped away in an instant. Salvation, on the other hand, comes with a guarantee that is personally signed and sealed by God. It guarantees us eternal life and God's active involvement in helping us acquire and retain the blessings He has reserved for us in this life.

God has amazing things in store for you. Now let's examine the Word of God together to ensure that you have taken the first step toward receiving every blessing God has for you.

PART 2

God's True Plan Of Salvation

*Peter said unto them, Repent, and be baptized every one of you in the name of
Jesus Christ for the remission of sins, and ye shall receive the
gift of the Holy Ghost.*

—Acts 2:38

CHAPTER 4

Simple Math

When God first spoke to me about the importance of writing this book, I knew I needed to communicate the biblical requirements for salvation with simplicity, so I wrote it as a simple equation.

Repentance

+

Water Baptism in the Name of Jesus Christ

+

Baptism of the Spirit

+

Faith

=

Salvation

As simple as the equation sounds, there are vital details of each component that must be explored. That is why we will closely examine each component of the equation separately.

As you read and study each of the following chapters, remember - we are in a war for souls. We cannot afford to lose even one. We must fight daily for our own souls and the souls of others. Salvation is the only way to win the war.

If you will diligently study the Bible and, in particular, the Scriptures you will find in this book, you will hear what God has said concerning salvation. When you hear it, you must decide whether or not to believe it. Finally, if you believe what you have heard, you must decide whether you will obey it. If you will do all three of those things, you will win the war for your own soul. If you will teach others to do the same, you will help them win the war for their souls.

Repentance

From that time Jesus began to preach, and to say, Repent: for the kingdom of heaven is at hand.

—Matthew 4:17

CHAPTER 5

Repentance Fables

There is only one thing that can separate us from God. That one thing is sin. Not just some sins, but all sin. That is why the journey to salvation begins in the same place for all of us. It begins with sincere repentance.

Repentance was the first message Jesus preached when He began His ministry. Throughout His ministry, repentance remained the central theme of His teachings. When He trained the twelve disciples and sent them out two by two, that is what He instructed them to preach. Mark 6:12 says this:

And they went out, and preached that men should repent.

Later, as the apostles continued the work Jesus began, repentance remained the focus of their message. One of the clearest examples of that message was delivered on the day of Pentecost.

On that day, many people made a mockery of those who had been filled with the Holy Ghost. However, when they realized that they had sinned against God, they asked Peter what they must do to be in right standing with Him. Peter's answer is recorded as follows in Acts 2:38:

> *Then Peter said unto them, Repent, and be baptized every one of you in the name of Jesus Christ for the remission of sins, and ye shall receive the gift of the Holy Ghost.*

Peter's response made it clear that repentance was the first step necessary for them to repair the breach they had caused in their relationship with God. Later, in Acts 5:30-31, Peter and the other apostles again addressed the importance of repentance when they reminded religious leaders why Jesus came to us:

> *The God of our fathers raised up Jesus, whom ye slew and hanged on a tree.*
>
> *Him hath God exalted with his right hand to be a Prince and a Saviour, for to give repentance to Israel, and forgiveness of sins.*

Unfortunately, as essential as it is, repentance is a terribly unpopular topic. It is unpopular because it brings us into conversations with God and with others about our sins. For most people, our own sin is a topic we desperately want to avoid. Nonetheless, sin is an issue that must be dealt with without hesitation or justification.

Addressing sin becomes easier when we recognize it for what it is. Sin is anything that separates and alienates us from God. Our sins may include our thoughts, speech, or actions. They may also include our failure to think, speak or act. When we fail to repent for whatever has alienated us from God, it is because we have fallen prey to the tricks and traps of the devil.

We must understand that we simply cannot allow ourselves to remain alienated from God under any circumstances. Instead, we must learn to embrace the gift of repentance that cleanses us of our sins and reconciles us to God. It becomes easier for us to receive the gift of repentance when we learn to recognize the tricks, traps, and fables concerning repentance. Let's begin by exploring some of the most common ones.

Fable: Ignorance is an acceptable excuse for sin.

Often we are simply unaware that many of the occasional or habitual things in our lives are, in fact, sins. We fall into the ignorance trap when we fail to repent because we do not recognize that we are in sin.

Unfortunately, ignorance about our sins does not exempt us from suffering the consequences of sin. The only way to overcome the ignorance trap is to study the Bible. The more we read and study, the more we will uncover hidden sins in our lives.

When we discover sins in our lives, we must change our thinking about them and accept that they are wrong in God's eyes. We must not only repent for our ignorance, we must also repent for the sin that resulted from our ignorance. After repenting, we must ask God to help us change.

Fable: I can afford this particular sin.

Another trap that keeps us from repenting is the pleasure trap. There are many sins that, quite frankly, we simply enjoy. We enjoy them so much that we truly have no desire or intention of changing. We believe that because those particular sins are so enjoyable, we can afford to keep them in our lives and we expect God to overlook them.

When we refuse to repent because we enjoy a particular sin, it is because we were lured into buying the sin without carefully examining the price tag. The price for all sin is the same. Romans 6:23 says this:

> For the wages of sin is death; but the gift of God is eternal life through Jesus Christ our Lord.

There are no cheap sins. This is no bargain rack. Sin is never on sale. All sin is exorbitantly priced and the pleasure is never worth the price.

Our pleasure sins are simply signed death warrants that we have chosen to purchase on credit. The bill will eventually come due, and when it does, someone will have to pay it. There are only two possibilities for who will pay the bill. Jesus will pay for it for those who sincerely repent and become counted as His sheep. Everyone else will pay their own bill.

Fable: God understands that I am just too ashamed of this particular sin to confess it and get the help that I need to overcome it.

Another trap many fall into is the shame trap. We often want to hide our sins from God. Like Adam and Eve, we find ourselves too ashamed to go to God or to others with a confession of our sins and a plea for help. Instead, we allow Satan to dupe us into believing that our sins are too great to be forgiven and too shameful to be openly discussed. Or, perhaps we believe that we have worn out our welcome with God by continually asking forgiveness for the same things.

Shame is a trick of the devil. He wants to cloak us in a blanket of shame and make us try to hide our sins from God. We cannot hide from God just as Adam and Eve could not hide from Him. God sees all of our sins and He desires to cleanse us of them. He wants to remove the blanket of shame and clothe us in His righteousness. God is ever faithful to forgive our sins.

The Bible tells us that blasphemy against the Holy Ghost is the only unforgivable sin. We must trust and believe that God can and will forgive us of all other sins. He never tires of our sincere efforts toward repentance and we cannot let the devil trick us into believing that He does.

God does not catalog, categorize, count, weigh, and measure all the varieties of sin in our lives as people often do. He understands that we all have our issues. We all have sin. We all need Jesus. That is why He died for us.

God deeply desires to forgive us for every single sin and He will – if we will repent. That is why the Bible makes us this faithful promise in 1 John 1:8-9:

> *If we say that we have no sin, we deceive ourselves, and the truth is not in us.*

> *If we confess our sins, he is faithful and just to forgive us our sins, and to cleanse us from all unrighteousness.*

God invites us to take every sin to Him for forgiveness, mercy, and help. In fact, Hebrews 4:16 tells us that God invites us to "come boldy unto the throne of grace, that we may obtain mercy, and find grace to help in time of need."

Does that sound like an invitation from a God who wants us to hide from Him in shame? No matter how long we struggle with a particular sin, we can boldly approach God with a repentant heart and ask for His help. God wants us to repent and He fully expects us to do so.

Fable: All God wants from me is an apology.

One of the most common fables is that repentance means that we simply apologize to God. Apologizing to God is a part of repentance. However, in addition to apologizing, God expects us to make a sincere and consistent effort to change.

Without a sincere, sustained effort to make a permanent change, we have not truly repented. We have only offered God an insincere apology for a sin we intend to continue. That leads us to another common fable that keeps many people from repenting from a sincere heart.

Fable: I can always sin now and repent later.

Many people have been lured into believing that they can sin now and repent later. In fact, I have often heard people jokingly and seriously express an intention to commit sins and repent later.

The truth is that when we willfully sin with the expressed intention of apologizing to God later, our planned repentance is not at all sincere. It is nothing more than an insincere apology to God that He may not accept. When we willfully sin, then offer God a half-hearted apology, we run the risk of having Him cut off our access to Him.

It is important for us to understand that our access to God is not a right to which we are entitled. It is a privilege that God extends to us at His discretion, but it is also a privilege He revokes at His discretion.

We cannot sin at will, then choose to repent whenever we feel like it. It is God who leads us to repentance when He tugs at our hearts to draw us back to Him. If God does not choose to lead us to repentance, the desire to repent will not be in our hearts and we will not repent.

We see this in Romans 2:4-6:

> *Or despisest thou the riches of his goodness and forbearance and longsuffering; not knowing that the goodness of God leadeth thee to repentance?*
>
> *But after thy hardness and impenitent heart treasurest up unto thyself wrath against the day of wrath and revelation of the righteous judgment of God;*
>
> *Who will render to every man according to his deeds:*

Jeremiah 15 gives us a frightening glimpse of God's heart toward those who continually return to their sins because their hearts are hardened toward Him. This is what He says in Jeremiah 15:6:

> *Thou hast forsaken me, saith the LORD, thou art gone backward: therefore will I stretch out my hand against thee, and destroy thee; I am weary with repenting.*

Instead of granting repentance, God turns many people over to a reprobate mind. This state of mind is described in Romans 1:28-32:

> *And even as they did not like to retain God in their knowledge, God gave them over to a reprobate mind, to do those things which are not convenient;*
>
> *Being filled with all unrighteousness, fornication, wickedness, covetousness, maliciousness; full of envy, murder, debate, deceit, malignity; whisperers,*
>
> *Backbiters, haters of God, despiteful, proud, boasters, inventors of evil things, disobedient to parents,*

Without understanding, covenantbreakers, without natural affection, implacable, unmerciful:

Who knowing the judgment of God, that they which commit such things are worthy of death, not only do the same, but have pleasure in them that do them.

When we continually toy with sin and God turns us over to a reprobate mind, we do not even recognize the need to repent. Our perception of sin becomes so distorted that we do not know the difference between right and wrong. Eventually, we are no longer conscious of the fact that we have been completely alienated from God. We do not recognize that we need to repent. When that occurs, not only will God not entertain our prayers, He will not even entertain the prayers of others on our behalf.

We see that truth in Jeremiah 14:10-12 which says:

Thus saith the LORD unto this people, Thus have they loved to wander, they have not refrained their feet, therefore the LORD doth not accept them; he will now remember their iniquity, and visit their sins.

Then said the LORD unto me, Pray not for this people for their good.

When they fast, I will not hear their cry; and when they offer burnt offering and an oblation, I will not accept them: but I will consume them by the sword, and by the famine, and by the pestilence.

This is why it is imperative that we continually offer sincere repentance to God when we find ourselves in sin. We should not choose to play with sin until we have had our fill of it and then attempt to repent later. It takes sincere repentance for us to maintain a relationship with God. The sincerity of our repentance is what keeps God's heart open to hearing our prayers and the prayers of others on our behalf.

Fable: I know what the Bible says, but that's not *really* a sin.

Perhaps the most dangerous trap of all is allowing the devil to lure us into believing that God has changed His absolute truths about sin. God does not change His mind about sin to accommodate our lifestyle choices or what we perceive to be more contemporary, enlightened spiritual truths.

Satan wants us to believe that as long as we call sin something other than sin, God will approve of it as an acceptable lifestyle, cultural norm, or legislated directive. That is not so. We cannot repackage our sins under new, more palatable labels and then present them to God as acceptable choices. We cannot legislate sins by erasing them from God's law and writing them into man's law.

Sin is still sin and truth is still truth. If God calls it a sin, it is a sin. No matter how we repackage, promote, or legislate sin, God still judges it in the same way. When sin comes before His throne for judgment, the price for new and improved, repackaged sin is the same as the price for old-fashioned sin. New labels for old sins do not change the price.

No matter what we hear, including from the pulpit, we must know with certainty that God says what He means and He means what He says – about everything. Numbers 23:19 says:

> *God is not a man, that he should lie; neither the son of man, that he should repent: hath he said, and shall he not do it? or hath he spoken, and shall he not make it good?*

If God calls it a sin, we cannot allow anyone to convince us otherwise. We must carefully examine our daily choices against the Word of God. We must recognize every sin in our lives. Most importantly, we must repent for all of our sins and lovingly help others to do the same.

Jesus came to call us out of sin and into a life of holiness for one reason. The Bible makes it abundantly clear that without holiness, no man shall see God. There is not one spot, blemish, wrinkle, or stain of sin that will make it into heaven, and there is not one spot, blemish, wrinkle, or stain of sin that can be removed without sincere repentance. Repentance was the first and central message in Jesus' ministry and it must remain the central theme in His Church. True repentance for every sin is our first step toward salvation.

CHAPTER 6

Journey Of A King's Heart

None of our sins surprise God and they should not surprise us. We all have known and unknown sins. We all have public and private sins. We all have sins that we commit occasionally and sins we struggle with habitually.

Romans 3:23 says "all have sinned, and come short of the glory of God." Most of us can accept that we are not perfect and that we have sins that we must overcome. Unfortunately, however, there are times in many of our lives when we stoop to levels of depravity that we never could have imagined. It is in those times that we learn unsettling truths about our own imperfect human hearts.

We discover that the heart of man is a terribly flawed navigation device. Within each of our hearts lies the capacity for great evil. When our souls are weak, we can become so intoxicated by sin that others wonder who we have become. Sometimes we can no longer even recognize ourselves. Even in the lives of people who deeply love and cherish God, we often find grievously unspeakable sins.

When we find ourselves in those situations, we often wonder if God can ever forgive us. We wonder if others can forgive us. We wonder if we can forgive ourselves. We wonder if we will ever be able to crawl out of the seemingly bottomless pit of shame, blame, and sorrow. Unfortunately, others may never forgive us and we may struggle to forgive ourselves, but God always desires to forgive us when we approach Him with a truly repentant heart.

Perhaps one of the best examples of heartfelt repentance is found in Psalm 51. It is the prayer King David offered to God as he mourned his great moral failures as a king and as a man. In Psalm 51:1-10, we see of a glimpse of the brokenness of David's heart:

Have mercy upon me, O God, according to thy lovingkindness: according unto the multitude of thy tender mercies blot out my transgressions.

Wash me throughly from mine iniquity, and cleanse me from my sin.

For I acknowledge my transgressions: and my sin is ever before me.

Against thee, thee only, have I sinned, and done this evil in thy sight: that thou mightest be justified when thou speakest, and be clear when thou judgest.

Behold, I was shapen in iniquity; and in sin did my mother conceive me.

Behold, thou desirest truth in the inward parts: and in the hidden part thou shalt make me to know wisdom.

Purge me with hyssop, and I shall be clean: wash me, and I shall be whiter than snow.

Make me to hear joy and gladness; that the bones which thou hast broken may rejoice.

Hide thy face from my sins, and blot out all mine iniquities.

Create in me a clean heart, O God; and renew a right spirit within me.

The story that led David to write this psalm is familiar to most. However, the path of sin that led to the story's great notoriety is worth revisiting because of what it teaches us about repentance.

The story began when King David spied Bathsheba, a beautiful married woman, bathing as he stood looking out his window. After allowing his lusts to consume him, David sent for her to be brought to him. Soon thereafter, she sent word to him that she was pregnant with his child. In an effort to cover his sin, David devised a plan that seemed like a sure solution to his problem.

He sent orders to have Bathsheba's husband, Uriah, brought home from war to sleep with her. David believed that surely a man who had been away at war would enjoy nothing more than the comfort of his wife's arms. He was certain that Uriah's marital relations with Bathsheba would serve to mask the paternity of the child she was carrying. However, David's plan failed miserably.

Uriah's loyalty to the king and his fellow soldiers proved to be greater than his desire for his wife. So, instead of sleeping with his wife, Uriah decided to sleep outside the king's door. He chose to sacrificially suffer along with his fellow soldiers who remained at war rather than enjoying the company of his lovely wife.

When David discovered that Uriah's loyalty had ruined his plans to cover his sin, he developed a new plan. He chose to cover the sin of adultery with the sin of murder.

David had Uriah remain another night while David personally penned a letter to Joab, a leader in his army. In the letter, David instructed Joab to put Uriah on the front lines of battle to ensure that he was killed. Then, he sent the sealed letter by Uriah's very own hands to be delivered to Joab.

The letter was delivered. Joab followed the instructions. As soon as Uriah was killed in battle as the king ordered, David married Bathsheba. It seemed that the king's sin was safely hidden from the eyes of the world. Then, David received a sobering message delivered to him from the mouth of God's prophet.

God sent the prophet Nathan to remind David that his sin was neither hidden nor was it forgotten. More importantly, it surely would not go unpunished.

God rendered swift judgment against David's house. The child born to David and Bathsheba died because of his sin and the further effects of God's judgments lingered throughout David's life. Eventually, David wrote Psalm 51 from the depths of a broken heart as he reflected on his great failure as a king and as a man.

When we peel the onion to examine all the layers of sin in this story, it is evident that David's sins were considerable. In the process of fulfilling the lusts of his flesh, he sinned against many people.

David sinned against himself and Bathsheba when he lusted after her. He sinned against those whom he enlisted in his scandal when he sent them to bring another man's wife to him. He sinned against Bathsheba when he, as the king, required her services in his bed. He sinned against Uriah by sleeping with his wife. Unfortunately, the trail of sin did not stop there.

David also sinned against the men he involved in his plan for deception when he had Uriah sent home to sleep with Bathsheba. He sinned against Uriah, Bathsheba, and the unborn child when he devised a plan to misrepresent the paternity of the child.

He sinned against Uriah when he rewarded Uriah's great loyalty by having him hand deliver his own death sentence. He sinned against Joab by having him orchestrate the execution of an innocent man. Finally, he sinned against his own unborn child who later died as a result of his father's sin.

Clearly, David sinned against many people. Yet, when he wrote Psalm 51, he did not name all the people against whom he had sinned. When David broke down in godly sorrow and lamented his sin, this is what he wrote in Psalm 51:4:

> *Against thee, thee only, have I sinned, and done this evil in thy sight:*

Certainly David understood how deeply he had damaged the hearts and souls of many other people. However, he was overwhelmed with sorrow because he understood that his greatest sin was not against man. His greatest sin was against God. David's heart was broken because of the great breach he had caused in the relationship that was most precious to him.

Eventually we all must recognize what David recognized. Our sins against others and even those sins we commit against ourselves are truly sins against God. More importantly, when we truly love God, we will do all that we can to repent so God can reconcile us to Him.

What I find most interesting about this story is not how David viewed himself, but how God viewed him. God chose David to become king long before the scandal that began with his lust for Bathsheba.

When God rejected Saul as king because of his rebellion, David was anointed to become his successor. This is the message God sent the prophet Samuel to deliver to Saul about the person chosen to replace him. 1 Samuel 13:14 says:

> *But now thy kingdom shall not continue: the LORD hath sought him a man after his own heart, and the LORD hath commanded him to be captain over his people, because thou hast not kept that which the LORD commanded thee.*

David? A man after God's own heart? It would seem that a man with the capacity for such great evil certainly could not also be a man after God's own heart. Yet, that is how God viewed David.

God knew even before David became king that his sin would lead to a monumentally scandalous story of lust, adultery, deception, and murder. He knew that people would talk about it, teach and preach about it, write books and make movies about it probably until the end of time.

So why did God choose a man like David to replace Saul? I believe we find the answer in Psalm 51. I am convinced that God chose David because, despite his capacity for great sin, he had a greater capacity for heartfelt repentance.

Sin is a fact of life. It always will be. God knows that sometimes we will stoop to moral lows that will shock us. When we do, we may find it difficult to reconcile in our minds the great sins in our lives with our great love for God. Thankfully, even our most shocking sins are not at all shocking to God.

God knew exactly what David would eventually do, yet He still chose him to be king. Like David, many of us have found ourselves deeply wounded by our own sins. Often our own sins leave us shocked, shattered, disillusioned, and deeply ashamed.

However, even when we find ourselves wallowing in the filth of our most shameful sins, God is still there. He still extends His hand to us in love and invites us to repent. When we do, He reaches down and lifts us out of our filth. He cleanses us and covers the shame of our nakedness. He clothes us in His righteousness and restores our dignity. He heals our hearts, restores the protections and provisions of our salvation, and gently guides us back into a right relationship with Him.

When we go to God with a repentant heart, He is faithful to forgive us. He is faithful to cleanse us and help us to change. If He did it for David, He will do it for you and for me.

No matter what sins we have committed, or how great or small we perceive them to be, there is never a good reason not to repent. Jesus Christ died to give us repentance and we should take full advantage of it as often as we need it.

Water Baptism
In The Name Of
Jesus Christ

*And he said unto them, Go ye into all the world, and preach the
gospel to every creature.*

*He that believeth and is baptized shall be saved; but he that
believeth not shall be damned.*

—Mark 16:15-16

CHAPTER 7

Water Baptism Fables

There are four key areas concerning water baptism that are vital to address. They relate to the requirement for baptism, the purpose of baptism, the method of baptism, and the name in which we are to be baptized.

REQUIREMENT FOR BAPTISM

Fable: Water baptism is not required for salvation.

Many people believe that water baptism is nothing more than an optional religious ceremony that is not required for salvation. However, there are many Scriptures that refute that belief. When addressing this particular fable, it is important to consider what Jesus did, examine what He said, then review additional Scriptures that lend further support to His message.

First and foremost, Jesus is a leader who led by example. He first did exactly what He expects us to do. Before beginning His public ministry, Jesus went to John the Baptist and insisted that John baptize Him. We see the record of His baptism in Matthew 3:13-17:

Then cometh Jesus from Galilee to Jordan unto John, to be baptized of him.

But John forbad him, saying, I have need to be baptized of thee, and comest thou to me?

And Jesus answering said unto him, Suffer it to be so now: for thus it becometh us to fulfil all righteousness. Then he suffered him.

And Jesus, when he was baptized, went up straightway out of the water: and, lo, the heavens were opened unto him, and he saw the Spirit of God descending like a dove, and lighting upon him:

And lo a voice from heaven, saying, This is my beloved Son, in whom I am well pleased.

When John the Baptist resisted Jesus' direction to baptize Him, Jesus was adamant that He must be baptized. Now that we have examined what Jesus did, let's examine what He said.

John 3:3-5 says:

Jesus answered and said unto him, Verily, verily, I say unto thee, Except a man be born again, he cannot see the kingdom of God.

Nicodemus saith unto him, How can a man be born when he is old? can he enter the second time into his mother's womb, and be born?

Jesus answered, Verily, verily, I say unto thee, Except a man be born of water and of the Spirit, he cannot enter into the kingdom of God.

Clearly, anyone who intends to enter into the kingdom of God must be born of water. Many people, however, insist that in this passage Jesus is referring to the water or amniotic fluid surrounding a fetus in the mother's womb. They teach that our natural birth fulfills the requirement stated in this passage.

That position, however, is not supported by the evidence we find in many other Scriptures. For example, consider what Jesus says in Mark 16:15-16:

And he said unto them, Go ye into all the world, and preach the gospel to every creature.

He that believeth and is baptized shall be saved; but he that believeth not shall be damned.

It is evident from this Scripture that Jesus states baptism is required for salvation. Further, it is evident that the baptism referenced is one that requires us to make a conscious choice to believe and be a willing participant. This eliminates the possibility that He is referring to amniotic fluid and our natural birth.

We find another example in 1 Peter 3:20-21. There, the Bible tells us that God used water to save the eight souls of Noah and his family and He now uses water baptism to save us. It says:

. . . when once the longsuffering of God waited in the days of Noah, while the ark was a preparing,wherein few, that is, eight souls were saved by water.

The like figure whereunto even baptism doth also now save us (not the putting away of the filth of the flesh, but the answer of a good conscience toward God,) by the resurrection of Jesus Christ:

We have established that, according to Jesus, we cannot enter into the kingdom of God without being born of water and of the Spirit. We have established that Jesus says we must believe and be baptized and, if we fail to believe, we will be damned. We have also seen that Peter, under the inspiration of the Holy Ghost, wrote that water saved the eight souls of Noah and his family just as water baptism now saves us.

Despite the clear record in the Bible indicating that baptism is required for our salvation, many people argue that Paul disagreed. Those individuals often cite a particular passage in 1 Corinthians in an effort to prove that Paul said something completely different than what Jesus said.

First, we must accept that the Bible does not contradict itself. Therefore, it is illogical for us to believe that Paul taught something that contradicts what Jesus taught. More importantly, it is illogical for us to believe that Paul knew more about the requirements for salvation than Jesus. Nonetheless, since it is frequently taught that Paul said baptism is not required for salvation, it is important for us to address that point.

First, let's consider what Paul said and then we will examine what he meant. In 1 Corinthians 1:14-17, Paul says the following:

> *I thank God that I baptized none of you, but Crispus and Gaius;*

> *Lest any should say that I had baptized in mine own name.*

> *And I baptized also the household of Stephanas: besides, I know not whether I baptized any other.*

> *For Christ sent me not to baptize, but to preach the gospel: not with wisdom of words, lest the cross of Christ should be made of none effect.*

Was Paul suggesting that baptism is not required for salvation? Absolutely not. When we examine the preceding verses, we gain a proper context for what he meant.

In the preceding verses of 1 Corinthians 1, Paul was admonishing believers about being contentious with each other. Divisions were being created among believers who were giving their allegiance to the person who had baptized them instead of recognizing that they all were to be united in Christ.

Paul recognized that because he was a prominent religious leader, it would have been easy for people to idolize him. He did not want to be the focus of attention among people who were boastful about having been personally baptized by him.

Instead, Paul wanted to ensure that people understood the importance of being baptized in the name of Jesus Christ alone. He wanted them to place their focus on Jesus Christ, not on him. We see that message in 1 Corinthians 1:13 where Paul asks:

> *Is Christ divided? was Paul crucified for you? or were ye baptized in the name of Paul?*

Paul's point in 1 Corinthians 1:14-17 is that he was thankful that he, personally, had not baptized a great number of people who could claim allegiance to him instead of to Jesus Christ. He was absolutely not dismissing the importance of baptism as a requirement for salvation.

In fact, in a later chapter we will examine Paul's own baptism experience. It will be evident from examining the events leading up to Paul's baptism that he clearly understood that baptism is required for salvation.

Another argument that many people use to suggest that baptism is not required for salvation is found in Luke 23:39-43 which says:

> *And one of the malefactors which were hanged railed on him, saying, If thou be Christ, save thyself and us.*

> *But the other answering rebuked him, saying, Dost not thou fear God, seeing thou art in the same condemnation?*

> *And we indeed justly; for we receive the due reward of our deeds: but this man hath done nothing amiss.*

> *And he said unto Jesus, Lord, remember me when thou comest into thy kingdom.*

> *And Jesus said unto him, Verily I say unto thee, Today shalt thou be with me in paradise.*

In this passage, we see that when Jesus was crucified, He promised one of the men on the cross next to Him that he would be with Him in paradise that very day. Many people assert that since this man was not baptized and Jesus received him, God will do the same for us if we choose not to be baptized.

First, let's be clear about the known facts of this particular story. The Bible does not state that this man was not baptized. That is an assumption. The Bible is silent on the issue.

What we do know is that baptism was a common practice. Through the ministry of John the Baptist, multitudes of people from all over the surrounding area flocked to the water to be baptized. His ministry, described in Matthew 3:1-17, was to preach repentance and baptize people to prepare them for the coming of the Lord. Matthew 3:5-6 says "Jerusalem, and all Judea, and all the region round about Jordan" went to him to be baptized and confess their sins.

Further, when Jesus began His ministry, He drew crowds of thousands of followers at a time. Many of these individuals were baptized. In fact, John 4:1-2 says that Jesus' disciples baptized even more people than John the Baptist.

Was the man on the cross one of those who chose to be baptized? He certainly could have been. Perhaps he first accepted Christ when he was baptized, but he, like many people, did not fully surrender his life to Jesus. Instead, he continued living in sin until he found himself hanging on a cross facing his last opportunity to repent. On the other hand, perhaps he was never baptized. Maybe the first time he put his hope in Jesus was when he was on his cross. The point is that we simply do not know whether he was baptized.

It is important to point out that the Bible is silent on this man's baptism so we know how to respond when he is used as an example to support the position that baptism is not required for salvation. However, there is a more important and frequently overlooked fact that makes the discussion of his baptism as it relates to salvation completely irrelevant.

The story of the man on the cross is found in the New Testament which causes many people to mistakenly believe that he was covered under the New Covenant. He was not. The New Covenant did not go into effect until *after* the death of Jesus Christ. Jesus' promise to the man on the cross took place *before* His death. Therefore, the man on the cross, in fact, died under the law of the Old Covenant.

What Jesus did for the man on the cross has absolutely nothing to do with us or a discussion about salvation. Jesus did something completely different for us. For us, Jesus Christ died on the cross and shed His blood so we can secure our salvation and gain entry into His kingdom under the New Covenant. Everyone who wants to be covered by the blood of the Lamb under the New Covenant must follow the instructions Jesus gave us.

Before His death and after His resurrection Jesus made it perfectly clear that if we want salvation and entry into the kingdom of God, we must be baptized in His name. He also made it clear that if we die after we have heard and willfully rejected the Gospel, we have no hope of salvation. This is the clear, unalterable message spoken from the mouth of Jesus Christ: "He that believeth and is baptized shall be saved; but he that believeth not shall be damned."

PURPOSE OF BAPTISM

Fable: Baptism is just a religious ceremony that allows us to publicly express our personal commitment to Jesus Christ.

We have already read what Jesus said concerning baptism and we know that damnation is the penalty for those who do not believe it. Damnation for failing to believe what Jesus said concerning baptism is a disturbingly harsh judgment that clearly should lead us to a serious question. Would Jesus condemn us to eternal damnation for failing to participate in a religious ceremony that is not required for salvation?

We can be certain that Jesus would only condemn us to eternal damnation for failing to do something He clearly told us is essential for our salvation. Our objective, then, is to understand why water baptism is so important to Jesus and why it should be equally important to us. Acts 2:38 gives us the answer. It says:

Peter said unto them, Repent, and be baptized every one of you in the name of Jesus Christ for the remission [forgiveness] of sins, and ye shall receive the gift of the Holy Ghost.

The process of establishing our salvation begins with repentance, but it does not end there. We also must be baptized in the name of Jesus Christ for our sins to be remitted or forgiven. Let's examine how that occurs.

There is only one thing that can redeem us and cleanse us of our sins. Ephesians 1:7 tells us what it is:

In whom we have redemption through his blood, the forgiveness of sins, according to the riches of his grace;

The precious blood of Jesus Christ is the inheritance that Jesus left us so we can be thoroughly cleansed, forgiven of our sins, and redeemed. Without the blood of Jesus we do not have salvation. Water baptism in the name of Jesus Christ is the method by which we receive our portion of that blood inheritance.

When God looks down from heaven as we are being baptized in the name of Jesus Christ, He doesn't see us covered in water. He sees us covered in that miracle working blood that Jesus shed on the cross. We will discuss later in this chapter how the water becomes blood. For now, however, let's examine Colossians 2:12-15 which gives us a clearer picture of what the blood of Jesus does for us when we are baptized in His name. It says:

Buried with him in baptism, wherein also ye are risen with him through the faith of the operation of God, who hath raised him from the dead.

And you, being dead in your sins and the uncircumcision of your flesh, hath he quickened together with him, having forgiven you all trespasses;

Blotting out the handwriting of ordinances that was against us, which was contrary to us, and took it out of the way, nailing it to his cross;

And having spoiled principalities and powers, he made a shew of them openly, triumphing over them in it.

When we are cleansed through baptism with our blood inheritance, God forgives our sins. He blots out the handwriting of all the ordinances that were against us, He takes them away, and nails them to the cross. However, that is not all that happens. Colossians 1:12-14 tells us more. It says:

Giving thanks unto the Father, which hath made us meet to be partakers of the inheritance of the saints in light:

Who hath delivered us from the power of darkness, and hath translated us into the kingdom of his dear Son:

In whom we have redemption through his blood, even the forgiveness of sins:

When we are baptized in the name of Jesus Christ, God redeems us by settling our debt. Remember all those sins that were blotted out and forgiven? There was a penalty for each and every one of them. The penalty is death and someone has to pay it. Until we are baptized in the name of Jesus Christ for the remission or forgiveness of our sins, we are responsible for paying the debt. However, once we are made partakers of the inheritance of the saints through the blood of Jesus Christ, His blood covers the entire bill.

Unfortunately, many believers today have not been properly taught the purpose of baptism so they do not obey the Word of God. They mistakenly believe that once they repent for their sins and accept Jesus as their Savior, by faith, they are covered by His blood and cleansed of their sins. As we have seen, this is not so.

When we repent and ask God to forgive us for our sins, we become believers of Jesus Christ. However, just as Jesus says in John 3:3-5, we do not enter into the kingdom of God as "born again" believers until we are born of water and of the Spirit. We have already read it, but it is well worth reading again:

Jesus answered and said unto him, Verily, verily, I say unto thee Except a man be born again, he cannot see the kingdom of God.

Nicodemus saith unto him, How can a man be born when he is old-?can he enter the second time into his mother's womb, and be born?

Jesus answered, Verily, verily, I say unto thee, Except a man be born of water and of the Spirit, he cannot enter into the kingdom of God.

That is why water baptism is so important to Jesus and why it must be equally important to us.

Fable: I receive the blood of Jesus by faith alone.

Many people find it difficult to believe that water turns to blood when they are baptized because their natural eyes cannot see the blood. Yet, they firmly believe that faith alone covers them under the blood even though their natural eyes cannot see it. The truth is that faith alone does not cover us under the blood of Jesus. Faith is only one of three elements required for us to be covered under the blood.

Colossians 2:12 tells us two of the elements. It says:

Buried with him in baptism, wherein also ye are risen with him through the faith of the operation of God, who hath raised him from the dead.

We see in this Scripture that we need water and we need faith of the operation (supernatural power) of God. The third element is the name of Jesus which we will discuss in a later section. When we go into the water and believe by faith that the name of Jesus will save us, the operation of God is activated to cover us under the blood.

For those who find this difficult to believe, it is important to examine the written record God left to build our faith. We see God's ability to transform the physical properties of water in Exodus 4:9 when He tells Moses to take water from the river, pour it on dry ground, and it will turn to blood. In

Exodus 7:17-25 God uses Moses to turn all the waters in Egypt including rivers, streams, and water in vessels into blood. All the fish die and all the water remains blood for seven days. In the very first miracle of His public ministry recorded in John 2 which we will explore later, Jesus turns water into wine.

So if the children of Israel saw the blood and the people at the wedding saw the wine, why can't we see the blood? If we could see it, we wouldn't need faith to believe it. And, as we have already seen in the Scripture, God requires faith in order for us to receive the blood.

It is so important that we understand how we receive the blood of Jesus because when we are sanctified by the blood, God also sanctifies our entire household. This is what 1 Corinthians 7:14 tells us:

> *For the unbelieving husband is sanctified by the wife, and the unbelieving wife is sanctified by the husband: else were your children unclean; but now are they holy.*

One of the best examples of entire households being covered by the blood is found in Exodus 12. God instructs Moses to have the children of Israel put the blood of a lamb on the two side posts and the upper door post of their homes. Nothing but the blood of the lamb can exempt their households from the tenth plague that is about to sweep through Egypt. When the death angel executes the plague by killing the firstborn of every household in Egypt including people and animals, beginning with Pharaoh's house, all the children of Israel are protected because of the blood.

Not one head of household says, "I believe by faith that my household is covered by the blood, so I choose not to kill a lamb and put the blood on my doorposts." To the contrary, everyone clearly understands the purpose of the blood. Everyone knows exactly how to get it. Everyone understands the absolute urgency of following every word of instruction spoken by Moses. Most importantly, everyone understands the consequences of failing to do so. The people clearly understand that failure to obey God's instruction surely will result in the death and destruction of their children.

This is why now, more so than ever, we must be diligent about ensuring that we are covered by the blood of Jesus. Our blood covering is essential for our own salvation and for the protection of our households, especially our children. Now that we understand the purpose of water baptism and how we receive the blood of Jesus, let's examine how God expects our baptisms to be performed.

METHOD OF BAPTISM

Fable: I can get baptized by having water sprinkled or poured on my head.

Jesus' baptism sets a clear standard for the proper method for water baptism. When Jesus was baptized, He was fully immersed, and then He rose out of the water. That is how He expects our water baptism to be performed. The entire body is to be fully immersed in water from head to toe. We see that in the definition given in Vine's Expository Dictionary for the Greek word used to describe Jesus' baptism. The word means "to dip repeatedly, to immerse, to submerge." Some churches, however, practice baptism by sprinkling or pouring water on one's head. That is not a proper water baptism.

Romans 6:3-9 shows us what occurs when we are baptized and why it is so important for us to be fully immersed in water. It says:

> *Know ye not, that so many of us as were baptized into Jesus Christ were baptized into his death?*
>
> *Therefore we are buried with him by baptism into death: that like as Christ was raised up from the dead by the glory of the Father, even so we also should walk in newness of life.*
>
> *For if we have been planted together in the likeness of his death, we shall be also in the likeness of his resurrection:*
>
> *Knowing this, that our old man is crucified with him, that the body of sin might be destroyed, that henceforth we should not serve sin.*

For he that is dead is freed from sin.

Now if we be dead with Christ, we believe that we shall also live with him:

Knowing that Christ being raised from the dead dieth no more; death hath no more dominion over him.

When we go down into the water in the name of Jesus Christ, we are baptized into His death. Our old man is crucified and our body of sin dies. What do we typically do with a dead body? We bury it. That is why the second verse of the passage says "we are buried with him." The water, which becomes the blood of Jesus, is the grave where we bury our dead body of sin.

I once heard a pastor explain that when we bury a corpse, we do not symbolically bury it by sprinkling or pouring dirt on its head. A corpse that is disposed of by sprinkling or pouring a little dirt on it will soon emit a stench so foul that no one will be able to bear it. It will continue to smell until it is fully buried in a grave or destroyed by fire through cremation.

The same is true of our body of sin. We do not symbolically baptize our body of sin by sprinkling or pouring water on it. Our body must be fully immersed in water so the body of sin can be destroyed. Only after we are completely buried in the blood of Jesus can we rise from the grave as a fully cleansed, brand new creation in Christ.

We have established that baptism is required for our salvation, and examined the purpose of baptism and the method by which we are to be baptized. Now, let's examine the significance of the name in which we are to be baptized.

THE NAME IN WHICH WE ARE TO BE BAPTIZED

Fable: We are to be baptized "in the name of the Father, and of the Son, and of the Holy Ghost [Holy Spirit]."

In Matthew 28:18-20, Jesus gives specific instructions concerning baptism. This is what He says:

And Jesus came and spake unto them, saying, All power is given unto me in heaven and in earth.

Go ye therefore, and teach all nations, baptizing them in the name of the Father, and of the Son, and of the Holy Ghost:

Teaching them to observe all things whatsoever I have commanded you: and, lo, I am with you alway, even unto the end of the world. Amen

Many people conclude from this passage that Jesus is instructing His disciples to recite the phrase "in the name of the Father, and of the Son, and of the Holy Ghost [Holy Spirit]" when baptisms are performed. Consequently, baptisms are often performed by saying something like, "I baptize you in the name of the Father, and of the Son, and of the Holy Spirit for the remission of sins."

However, that is not how the apostles baptized. None of the baptisms recorded in the New Testament were performed in the name of the Father, and of the Son, and of the Holy Ghost [Holy Spirit]. The apostles baptized in the name of Jesus Christ for the remission of sins.

Why is that?

It is because the apostles understood exactly what Jesus meant. They understood that Jesus expected them to use a specific name. Let's begin by examining those three verses more closely to see how we arrive at that conclusion.

If we were to look only at the second verse in that passage, we might reasonably conclude that Jesus is instructing his disciples to baptize "in the name of the Father, and of the Son, and of the Holy Ghost [Holy Spirit]." However, we see in the first verse that Jesus is speaking specifically about Himself. He states that *He* is the one with all power in heaven and in earth.

As we move to the second verse, we find two key words. The first word is "therefore." The word "therefore" is a transitional word used to direct our attention back to a point that was previously established. It signifies that the last point provides foundational support or justification for the point that is about to be made.

After Jesus establishes that He has all power in heaven and in earth, He follows that statement with, "Go ye *therefore*" and teach and baptize in a particular name. The second key word is "name." Jesus is clear that He is not instructing them to use multiple "names." He is instructing them to use a single name.

The name that Jesus instructs his disciples to use is the *name* of the Father, and of the Son, and of the Holy Ghost. That name is Jesus Christ. Jesus tells His disciples to teach and baptize in the *name* of Jesus Christ because He is the one with all power in heaven and in earth. That is why they used His name for baptisms.

Finally, in the third verse, Jesus again reminds them to *teach* all nations all that He commanded. That is why, as we see in Acts 2:38, Peter followed Jesus' instructions by *teaching* that we are to baptize *in the name of Jesus Christ* for the remission of sins. Let's examine the record to find further support.

There are two compelling perspectives that give us a clear understanding of who Jesus is, the fullness of His power and authority, and the importance of using His name. The first perspective comes from Jesus and His followers. The second perspective which is equally compelling comes from His enemies who also clearly understood the power of His name. In fact, their understanding of the power of the name of Jesus is what led to the great persecution of the apostles and the early Church.

In order for us to fully appreciate the perspective of Jesus and His followers, we must first understand the Godhead. The Godhead is comprised of the Father, and of the Son, and of the Holy Spirit. However, as we have seen in Matthew 28:19, Jesus says there is a *name* associated with the Godhead which we are to use for baptism. In Colossians, we find the name. Colossians 2:9-15 tells us that Jesus Christ is the bodily representation of the Godhead and we are complete in *Him*:

For in him [Christ] dwelleth all the fulness of the Godhead bodily.

And ye are complete in him, which is the head of all principality and power:

In whom also ye are circumcised with the circumcision made without hands, in putting off the body of the sins of the flesh by the circumcision of Christ:

Buried with him in baptism, wherein also ye are risen with him through the faith of the operation of God, who hath raised him from the dead.

And you, being dead in your sins and the uncircumcision of your flesh, hath he quickened together with him, having forgiven you all trespasses;

Blotting out the handwriting of ordinances that was against us, which was contrary to us, and took it out of the way, nailing it to his cross;

And having spoiled principalities and powers, he made a shew of them openly, triumphing over them in it.

We have established that Jesus has all power in heaven and in earth and that He instructs us to use His name for baptism. Additionally, we have established that in Him dwells the fullness and complete power and authority of the Godhead. So, how do we access His power? Let's examine what the Bible teaches us in Philippians 2:5-11 about His name. It says:

Let this mind be in you, which was also in Christ Jesus:

Who, being in the form of God, thought it not robbery to be equal with God:

But made himself of no reputation, and took upon him the form of a servant, and was made in the likeness of men:

And being found in fashion as a man, he humbled himself, and became obedient unto death, even the death of the cross.

Wherefore God also hath highly exalted him, and given him a name which is above every name:

That at the name of Jesus every knee should bow, of things in heaven, and things in earth, and things under the earth;

And that every tongue should confess that Jesus Christ is Lord, to the glory of God the Father.

Here we see that all the power Jesus possesses is contained in one place – His name. Finally, let's examine what Jesus says concerning His name. In John 17, we find Jesus' prayer to His Father just before He was crucified. This is what He said in John 17:4-6:

I have glorified thee on the earth: I have finished the work which thou gavest me to do.

And now, O Father, glorify thou me with thine own self with the glory which I had with thee before the world was.

I have manifested thy name unto the men which thou gavest me out of the world: thine they were, and thou gavest them me; and they have kept thy word.

In His prayer, Jesus tells His Father that He has finished His work which is to glorify His Father by manifesting *His Father's name* on earth. This is how He concludes that prayer in the last verse of John 17:

And I have declared unto them thy name, and will declare it: that the love wherewith thou hast loved me may be in them, and I in them.

Jesus does not say, "I have declared unto them *my* name." He says, "I have declared unto them *thy* name." Jesus understands that the name He was given is His Father's name. We must understand that, likewise, we must take His name. We do so by being baptized in the *name* of Jesus Christ for the remission of our sins.

All the Scriptures we have examined thus far certainly make a compelling case for why we must use the name of Jesus Christ for baptisms. However, some of the most compelling evidence we find in support of using His name comes not from Jesus or His followers, but from His adversaries.

Nowhere is this more evident than in Acts 4 and 5. In these two chapters, we discover that the religious leaders were fiercely angered by the apostles' great demonstrations of power. After watching the miracles performed by the apostles, including the notable healing of a lame man, they clearly understood that there is a name by which the apostles were able to perform such miracles. In Acts 4:7 we see that they finally demanded an answer to the question that was burning in their hearts:

> *By what power, or by what name, have ye done this?*

This is how Peter responded in Acts 4:8-12:

> *Then Peter, filled with the Holy Ghost, said unto them, Ye rulers of the people, and elders of Israel,*
>
> *If we this day be examined of the good deed done to the impotent man, by what means he is made whole;*
>
> *Be it known unto you all, and to all the people of Israel, that by the name of Jesus Christ of Nazareth, whom ye crucified, whom God raised from the dead, even by him doth this man stand here before you whole.*
>
> *This is the stone which was set at nought of you builders, which is become the head of the corner.*

> *Neither is there salvation in any other: for there is none other name under heaven given among men, whereby we must be saved.*

Peter gave them the name they wanted to know. The lame man was made whole by the name of Jesus Christ of Nazareth.

Once the religious leaders got their answer, Acts 4:14-18 tells us how they responded. It says:

> *And beholding the man which was healed standing with them, they could say nothing against it.*
>
> *But when they had commanded them to go aside out of the council, they conferred among themselves,*
>
> *Saying, What shall we do to these men? for that indeed a notable miracle hath been done by them is manifest to all them that dwell in Jerusalem; and we cannot deny it.*
>
> *But that it spread no further among the people, let us straitly threaten them, that they speak henceforth to no man in this name.*
>
> *And they called them, and commanded them not to speak at all nor teach in the name of Jesus.*

The religious leaders knew they could not deny the power, nor could they destroy it. Even after crucifying Jesus, great demonstrations of His power continued to manifest when His name was used. The only thing they could do was attempt to suppress His power by silencing the use of His name.

Despite the threats, the apostles refused to yield to their demands. Peter and John's response to them is recorded in Acts 4:19-20 which says:

> *But Peter and John answered and said unto them, Whether it be right in the sight of God to hearken unto you more than unto God, judge ye.*

For we cannot but speak the things which we have seen and heard.

The apostles continued preaching and teaching in the name of Jesus Christ. The great demonstrations of power continued, and the persecution escalated. As we see later, the apostles were hauled in again and reprimanded by the high priest for using the name of Jesus Christ. Acts 5:27-28 says:

> *And when they had brought them, they set them before the council: and the high priest asked them,*
>
> *Saying, Did not we straitly command you that ye should not teach in this name? and, behold, ye have filled Jerusalem with your doctrine, and intend to bring this man's blood upon us.*

Still, the apostles' response did not change. Acts 5:29-32 tells us that they held fast to their belief in the name of Jesus and refused to back down. It says:

> *Then Peter and the other apostles answered and said, We ought to obey God rather than men.*
>
> *The God of our fathers raised up Jesus, whom ye slew and hanged on a tree.*
>
> *Him hath God exalted with his right hand to be a Prince and a Saviour, for to give repentance to Israel, and forgiveness of sins.*
>
> *And we are his witnesses of these things; and so is also the Holy Ghost, whom God hath given to them that obey him.*

One of the most notable examples of the response to the name of Jesus is found in Acts 19:13-20. It says:

Then certain of the vagabond Jews, exorcists, took upon them to call over them which had evil spirits the name of the Lord Jesus, saying, We adjure you by Jesus whom Paul preacheth.

And there were seven sons of one Sceva, a Jew, and chief of the priests, which did so.

And the evil spirit answered and said, Jesus I know, and Paul I know; but who are ye?

And the man in whom the evil spirit was leaped on them, and over-came them, and prevailed against them, so that they fled out of that house naked and wounded.

And this was known to all the Jews and Greeks also dwelling at Ephesus; and fear fell on them all, and the name of the Lord Jesus was magnified.

And many that believed came, and confessed, and shewed their deeds.

Many of them also which used curious arts brought their books to-gether, and burned them before all men: and they counted the price of them, and found it fifty thousand pieces of silver.

So mightily grew the word of God and prevailed.

The evil spirit's reaction to the name of Jesus was so compelling that even those who practiced magic and other forms of the occult became believers in Jesus Christ and publicly burned their books.

There is *power* in the *name* of Jesus. That is why Jesus gave us a simple instruction concerning baptism. We are to use His name because His name alone has the power to change the plain water we use for baptism into the blood of Jesus.

In the very first miracle of Jesus' public ministry, He turned water into wine just as He turns baptismal water into blood. The story is recorded in John 2:1-11:

And the third day there was a marriage in Cana of Galilee; and the mother of Jesus was there:

And both Jesus was called, and his disciples, to the marriage.

And when they wanted wine, the mother of Jesus saith unto him, They have no wine.

Jesus saith unto her, Woman, what have I to do with thee? mine hour is not yet come.

His mother saith unto the servants, Whatsoever he saith unto you, do it.

And there were set there six waterpots of stone, after the manner of the purifying of the Jews, containing two or three firkins apiece.

Jesus saith unto them, Fill the waterpots with water. And they filled them up to the brim.

And he saith unto them, Draw out now, and bear unto the governor of the feast. And they bare it.

When the ruler of the feast had tasted the water that was made wine, and knew not whence it was: (but the servants which drew the water knew;) the governor of the feast called the bridegroom,

And saith unto him, Every man at the beginning doth set forth good wine; and when men have well drunk, then that which is worse: but thou hast kept the good wine until now.

This beginning of miracles did Jesus in Cana of Galilee, and manifested forth his glory; and his disciples believed on him.

There is an important principle that we all can learn from this story. Let's examine it.

Mary saw a problem and she knew her Son had the power to solve it. She also knew with certainty that He was willing to do so, though He initially resisted her request. Most importantly, Mary knew exactly how to get that miracle from Jesus. We see it in this clear, unapologetic directive she gives the servants:

His mother saith unto the servants, Whatsoever he saith unto you, do it.

Jesus gave the simple instruction and the servants brought the water. Jesus didn't move from His seat. He didn't touch the water. He didn't touch the waterpots. He didn't speak to the water or to the waterpots. Yet, in an instant, His mere presence miraculously transformed the physical properties of that plain water, turning it into the finest wine. The servants were able to serve wine to the wedding guests because they obeyed Jesus' simple instruction. Had they failed to do so, they would have been serving plain water.

This is the principle. We all have problems and Jesus always has the answer. Depending on the nature of our problem, a miracle may be required to solve it. Our ability to receive the answers and miracles we need from Jesus is dependent upon our willingness to hear, believe, and obey His simple instructions. When we do exactly what Jesus instructs us to do, He will perform whatever miracle is necessary to solve our problem.

The one problem we all have in common is that we are born in sin. As long as we remain in sin, we have restricted access to God's blessings. We cannot enter into the kingdom of God and we cannot pass through the gates of heaven. The one miracle we all need to solve our sin problem is a way to gain access to the blood of Jesus. The simple instruction we must follow to receive His blood is that we must be baptized in water, believe by faith that His name has the power to save us, and use the name of Jesus for our baptism.

When we do, Jesus will cleanse us with His blood and He will sanctify our households.

Many churches perform baptisms "in the name of the Father, and of the Son, and of the Holy Spirit." Those baptisms have missed the mark.

Other churches, for various reasons, baptize by combining the phrases "in the name of the Father, and of the Son, and of the Holy Spirit" and "in the name of Jesus Christ." Some do so to accommodate individuals who wish to maintain the tradition of being baptized in the name of the Father, and of the Son, and of the Holy Spirit. Some do so out of uncertainty about whether to baptize according to Matthew 28:19 or Acts 2:38. Others recognize the mandate to baptize in the name of Jesus Christ, but also desire to incorporate wording from Matthew 28:19.

There is absolute power and perfection in a full-immersion baptism when it is performed in the name of Jesus Christ. We cannot perfect a baptism without using His name. We cannot improve upon perfection by adding words to His name. If we are to return to the precise standard for baptism used by the apostles in response to the instruction they received from Jesus Christ, we only need to baptize in the name of Jesus Christ for the remission of sins because we are complete in Him.

If you have never been baptized, it is time to do so. If you were baptized, but not in the *name* of Jesus Christ, read Acts 19:1-5. It provides a clear record of what to do. Get baptized again – this time in the name of Jesus Christ for the remission of your sins. If you are unsure of how you were previously baptized, get baptized again. It's always better to be safe than sorry.

Baptism Of The Spirit

But ye are not in the flesh, but in the Spirit, if so be that the Spirit of God dwell in you. Now if any man have not the Spirit of Christ, he is none of his.

—*Romans 8:9*

CHAPTER 8

The Adoption Process

I wish we were finished uncovering all the salvation related fables. Unfortunately, we have only uncovered the tip of the iceberg. Baptism of the Spirit is a topic that is richly embellished with many deeply rooted fables. It is also the area where, in my experience, people become the most defensive and resistant to biblical truth.

The truth on this subject is often met with such resistance because it challenges many people's well established belief systems about their relationship with God. When people who believe that they have God's Spirit learn that, according to the Bible, they do not, they are often deeply disturbed, shocked, angry, and even downright offended. When we find ourselves experiencing these emotions, we often harden our hearts to the truth.

Nonetheless, despite how disruptive the truth on this subject may be, we must dig into the Word to find it. More importantly, we must embrace it. Romans 8:11 tells us why. It says:

> But if the Spirit of him that raised up Jesus from the dead dwell in you, he that raised up Christ from the dead shall also quicken your mortal bodies by his Spirit that dwelleth in you.

It is God's Spirit that provided the resurrection power that raised Jesus from the dead and that same Spirit will raise us from the dead, too. However, until we receive the baptism of the Spirit, we do not have God's Spirit. If we do not have His Spirit, we have no resurrection power, and we have no hope of heaven.

That is why it is imperative that we examine each fable related to being born of the Spirit, one by one, in detail, until we arrive at the whole truth. Only then can we truly determine if we have received God's Spirit which has the resurrection power that will quicken us and raise us from the dead.

However, before we examine new truths that uproot deeply rooted fables, I believe it is important to first prepare people's hearts to receive the truth. Luke 8 tells us that the seeds of God's Word must be sown in the good ground of a fertile heart that can receive the seed.

Uprooting foundational beliefs can deeply wound people. When hearts are wounded, they often become hardened, stony ground where seeds of truth cannot take root and flourish.

The first and most important thing we all must understand is that God loves us. He loves us enough that He sent His only begotten Son to die for us. 1 John 3:1 says, "Behold, what manner of love the Father hath bestowed upon us, that we should be called the sons of God."

However, as much as God desires for us to be His children, we are not born as children of God. We are all born as sinners who are alienated from God and estranged from His kingdom as we see in Ephesians 2:10-19 which says:

> *For we are his workmanship, created in Christ Jesus unto good works, which God hath before ordained that we should walk in them.*
>
> *Wherefore remember, that ye being in time past Gentiles in the flesh, who are called Uncircumcision by that which is called the Circumcision in the flesh made by hands;*

That at that time ye were without Christ, being aliens from the commonwealth of Israel, and strangers from the covenants of promise, having no hope, and without God in the world:

But now in Christ Jesus ye who sometimes were far off are made nigh by the blood of Christ.

For he is our peace, who hath made both one, and hath broken down the middle wall of partition between us;

Having abolished in his flesh the enmity, even the law of commandments contained in ordinances; for to make in himself of twain one new man, so making peace;

And that he might reconcile both unto God in one body by the cross, having slain the enmity thereby:

And came and preached peace to you which were afar off, and to them that were nigh.

For through him we both have access by one Spirit unto the Father.

Now therefore ye are no more strangers and foreigners, but fellow-citizens with the saints, and of the household of God;

In order for us to shed our status as strangers and foreigners and become members of the household of God, we all must go through God's adoption process. We see that in Galatians 4:4-5 which says:

But when the fulness of the time was come, God sent forth his Son, made of a woman, made under the law,

To redeem them that were under the law, that we might receive the adoption of sons.

Our adoption cannot be finalized and sealed until we receive God's Spirit through the baptism of the Spirit. Only when our adoption is complete are we fully established in the kingdom of God. So, what is the adoption process?

The adoption process begins when we choose Jesus Christ as our Lord, repent for our sins, and place our faith in Him as our Savior. That is when we are first converted in our hearts. Next, we must be cleansed of our sins through water baptism in His name, and be filled with God's Spirit through the baptism of the Spirit.

Just as with natural adoptions, the length of the process varies on a case by case basis. For some, it is a gradual process. For others, it occurs in a sudden, dramatic, life changing experience.

If your adoption is not complete because you have not yet received the baptism of the Spirit, you must trust and believe that God loves you. He has not rejected you. He has chosen you and He desires to fill you with His Spirit. Trust and believe that God is more excited about finalizing your adoption than you are!

Luke 11:9-13 clearly tells us that God will not withhold His Spirit from those who ask Him for it. It says:

> *And I say unto you, Ask, and it shall be given you; seek, and ye shall find; knock, and it shall be opened unto you.*

> *For every one that asketh receiveth; and he that seeketh findeth; and to him that knocketh it shall be opened.*

> *If a son shall ask bread of any of you that is a father, will he give him a stone? or if he ask a fish, will he for a fish give him a serpent?*

> *Or if he shall ask an egg, will he offer him a scorpion?*

> *If ye then, being evil, know how to give good gifts unto your children: how much more shall your heavenly Father give the Holy Spirit to them that ask him?*

Ask God for His Spirit, then seek Him diligently in prayer and wait for Him to give it to you.

Ezekiel 36:25-28 tells us of God's plan to cleanse us with water, give us a new heart and a new spirit, and adopt us. In Ephesians 1:3-14, God again reinforces that He has chosen us to be His. Ephesians 1:13 specifically tells us that God seals our adoption or redemption with His Spirit. Galatians 4:4-7 speaks further about our adoption. Acts 5:32 promises that God will give His Spirit to those who obey Him. Believe God!

If you have not yet received the baptism of the Spirit and you eagerly desire it, trust that one day soon God will pour out His Spirit on you. In the meantime, remember - no matter how long it takes, every child who is waiting for their adoption to be finalized should rejoice in knowing that they have already been chosen. It is not a question of love, acceptance, or approval. It is only a matter of time. We must trust God's timing and allow Him to take us through the necessary preparations to receive His Spirit.

CHAPTER 9

Baptism Of The Spirit Fables

There are several fables concerning what it means to be born of the Spirit that are important for us to uproot before we plant the truth. I believe it is as important to use the Word of God to uproot fables as it is to use it to plant the truth. So, once again, let's begin by uprooting some of the most common fables.

Fable: We are all God's children.

One common fable we frequently encounter is the belief that we are all God's children. It is true that we are all God's creations; however, we are not all God's children.

If you doubt that to be true, there is an interesting conversation in John 8:12-59 between Jesus and the Pharisees that I encourage you to read. Jesus was talking to them about the truth that He was teaching which they had rejected. After rejecting the truth, they insisted in John 8:41 that God was their Father.

This is what Jesus said when He corrected them in John 8:42-44:

Jesus said unto them, If God were your Father, ye would love me: for I proceeded forth and came from God; neither came I of myself, but he sent me.

Why do ye not understand my speech? even because ye cannot hear my word.

Ye are of your father the devil, and the lusts of your father ye will do. He was a murderer from the beginning, and abode not in the truth, because there is no truth in him. When he speaketh a lie, he speaketh of his own: for he is a liar, and the father of it.

From this conversation, we can be certain of two things: Jesus is not of the opinion that we are all God's children, nor is He of the opinion that all religious leaders are God's children. In fact, He pointedly tells these particular religious leaders that their father is the devil.

Fable: We all have God's Spirit.

Everyone is not considered God's child because not everyone has God's Spirit. We see that truth in Romans 8:9 which says:

But ye are not in the flesh, but in the Spirit, if so be that the Spirit of God dwell in you. Now if any man have not the Spirit of Christ, he is none of his.

This clearly tells us that there are people who do not have God's Spirit. It is true that we all are born with a spirit, but we are not born with God's Spirit. We do not receive God's Spirit, which is the Spirit of Christ, until God fills us with it through the baptism of the Spirit.

Fable: I can tell who has God's Spirit by observing behavior.

This particular fable is best examined in Galatians 5:14-23 in the context of the works of the flesh and the fruit of the Spirit. This is what it says:

For all the law is fulfilled in one word, even in this; Thou shalt love thy neighbour as thyself.

But if ye bite and devour one another, take heed that ye be not consumed one of another.

This I say then, Walk in the Spirit, and ye shall not fulfil the lust of the flesh.

For the flesh lusteth against the Spirit, and the Spirit against the flesh: and these are contrary the one to the other: so that ye cannot do the things that ye would.

But if ye be led of the Spirit, ye are not under the law.

Now the works of the flesh are manifest, which are these; Adultery, fornication, uncleanness, lasciviousness,

Idolatry, witchcraft, hatred, variance, emulations, wrath, strife, seditions, heresies,

Envyings, murders, drunkenness, revellings, and such like: of the which I tell you before, as I have also told you in time past, that they which do such things shall not inherit the kingdom of God.

But the fruit of the Spirit is love, joy, peace, longsuffering, gentleness, goodness, faith,

Meekness, temperance: against such there is no law.

After reading that passage, people often conclude that individuals who consistently demonstrate the works of the flesh do not have God's Spirit. Conversely, they believe that those who consistently demonstrate behaviors that look like the fruit of the Spirit *do* have God's Spirit. That is not necessarily true.

Often, people who are not filled with God's Spirit have a pleasant temperament, nice manners, and good interpersonal skills. They show love to others through their behaviors and are often a genuine pleasure to be around.

Their behaviors look like what we would hope to see in someone who is filled with God's Spirit. However, their ability to demonstrate those behaviors does not necessarily mean that they have been filled with God's Spirit.

We also encounter people with an unpleasant temperament and poor social skills who are often rude, abrasive, and have other obvious struggles with sin that make them unpleasant to be around. We might assume that these individuals could not possibly have God's Spirit, but this is not necessarily so.

Some of these individuals may very well be filled with God's Spirit. Yet, despite being filled with His Spirit, perhaps God has not yet healed their hearts sufficiently for the fruit of the Spirit to be evident in their character.

Even after being filled with the Spirit, we all continue to wrestle with sin. Some of us wrestle privately with sins that are not evident to others. Some of us struggle with sins that manifest in unpleasant behaviors that are often offensive to others.

Our common struggle with sin is evident in Romans 7:14-25 which was written by the apostle Paul. In that passage, he says the following concerning the struggle with sin:

> *For we know that the law is spiritual: but I am carnal, sold under sin.*

> *For that which I do I allow not: for what I would, that do I not; but what I hate, that do I.*

> *If then I do that which I would not, I consent unto the law that it is good.*

> *Now then it is no more I that do it, but sin that dwelleth in me.*

For I know that in me (that is, in my flesh,) dwelleth no good thing: for to will is present with me; but how to perform that which is good I find not.

For the good that I would I do not: but the evil which I would not, that I do.

Now if I do that I would not, it is no more I that do it, but sin that dwelleth in me.

I find then a law, that, when I would do good, evil is present with me.

For I delight in the law of God after the inward man:

But I see another law in my members, warring against the law of my mind, and bringing me into captivity to the law of sin which is in my members.

O wretched man that I am! who shall deliver me from the body of this death?

I thank God through Jesus Christ our Lord. So then with the mind I myself serve the law of God; but with the flesh the law of sin.

We see that even Paul who certainly had God's Spirit acknowledged that we continually wrestle with the sin that dwells within us. Some struggles may be private, while other struggles may be evident to those around us. Therefore, it is imperative to recognize that outward behavior only demonstrates our level of victory over sin. It cannot be used to conclusively determine whether someone has God's Spirit.

Fable: I know I have God's Spirit because I feel His presence.

People often believe that they have God's Spirit because they feel His presence and have had spiritual encounters with Him. Many people describe experiences with God that give them chills or goose bumps. They often believe that God has touched them in a meaningful way and, quite often, they are right. Perhaps they have had a deeply meaningful encounter with God's Spirit. However, that does not mean they have been born of the Spirit.

God uses spiritual encounters with us to draw us closer to Him. He uses them to make us aware of His power and His presence and to encourage us to draw into a deeper relationship with Him.

There is a great distinction, however, between sensing and perceiving God's presence, and being filled with His Spirit. We must remember that God created the heavens and the earth. He can and does communicate with and give direction to everything He created including people, animals, everything in nature, angels, demons, and even Satan himself.

The Bible provides many examples of spiritual encounters God had with people, animals, and things that are not filled with His Spirit. In Numbers 22, God allowed a donkey to perceive spiritual things. Later, in 1 Kings 17, He communicated with ravens and gave them the task of taking food to Elijah twice a day.

Job 1 shows us that Satan stood among the sons of God and conversed with God. In Mark 4, Jesus commanded the wind and the waves to be still and they obeyed His command. In Mark 5, He cast demons out of a man and gave them permission to enter into a herd of swine.

Clearly, everything and everyone hears God and is subject to His authority. However, just because a person, spiritual being, animal, or element of nature hears and responds to God does not mean that it is filled with God's Spirit.

When we have a spiritual encounter with God, He is on the outside of us, speaking to us, or interacting with us. However, when we receive the baptism of the Spirit, God fills us with His Spirit and He speaks to us from within.

Ephesians 3:17 tells us that Jesus Christ literally moves from the outside of us and He personally comes to dwell within us. We must understand that God may draw us in with spiritual encounters, but He may not actually fill us with His Spirit until much later.

Fable: We are automatically filled with God's Spirit as soon as we repent for our sins and invite Jesus Christ to come into our hearts.

Unfortunately, for many people, this particular fable has become the foundation of their faith. They have embraced it as the core truth about how their relationship with Jesus Christ was established. That is why it is so difficult for many people to accept that it is, indeed, a fable.

Countless people who have confessed Jesus Christ as their Savior have been taught that all we must do to establish our salvation is say a prayer of repentance. That prayer, often referred to as the Sinner's Prayer of Salvation, is taken from Romans 10:9-10 which we will examine closely in a later chapter. When we pray that prayer, we ask God to forgive us of our sins and we invite Jesus Christ into our hearts. Unfortunately, many new believers are told that praying that prayer establishes them in the kingdom of God as born again believers who are filled with God's Spirit.

That simply is not true. Certainly, we must do all of those things to receive Jesus as our Savior. However, we do not automatically receive His Spirit by doing these things, nor do we automatically enter into the kingdom of God. This is a terribly disruptive truth about salvation for many people. Nonetheless, we find proof of it in several places in the Bible.

One of the clearest examples is in Acts 9 where we find the conversion experience of Saul of Tarsus who later became known as the apostle Paul. We will examine this story in greater detail in a later chapter. For now, we will use it to show that we do not automatically receive the infilling of God's Spirit when we repent and accept Jesus Christ as Lord. This is what Acts 9:3-6 says:

> *And as he [Saul] journeyed, he came near Damascus: and suddenly there shined round about him a light from heaven:*

> *And he fell to the earth, and heard a voice saying unto him, Saul, Saul, why persecutest thou me?*

And he said, Who art thou, Lord? And the Lord said, I am Jesus whom thou persecutest: it is hard for thee to kick against the pricks.

And he trembling and astonished said, Lord, what wilt thou have me to do? And the Lord said unto him, Arise, and go into the city, and it shall be told thee what thou must do.

We see from the text that Saul clearly believed in Jesus after this encounter. In fact, Saul confessed Jesus as Lord, he willingly surrendered to Jesus, and obeyed the instructions Jesus gave him. However, we learn later in Acts 9:17 that Saul did not receive the Holy Ghost until three days after that encounter with Jesus when he was visited by a man named Ananias. This is what Acts 9:17 says about the meeting between Saul and Ananias:

And Ananias went his way, and entered into the house; and putting his hands on him said, Brother Saul, the Lord, even Jesus, that appeared unto thee in the way as thou camest, hath sent me, that thou mightest receive thy sight, and be filled with the Holy Ghost.

Few people have had an experience with Jesus that is as life altering as Saul's experience on the road to Damascus. He saw a light come down from heaven and shine on him. He heard the audible voice of Jesus Christ personally speak to him. Everyone who was with him heard the voice. The presence of the Spirit of Jesus Christ was so powerful that Saul was left trembling and astonished. Not only did he have a dramatic spiritual encounter, he departed from that encounter with a physical manifestation that left him blind for three days. Yet, after that undeniably powerful experience with Jesus Christ, Saul still did not receive the Holy Ghost.

If it were true that we are automatically filled with God's Spirit when we repent and confess Jesus Christ as Lord, Saul surely would have received the infilling of the Holy Ghost while on the road to Damascus. However, the text shows us that he did not receive the baptism of the Spirit until three days later.

Based on that example alone, we can reasonably conclude that we do not automatically receive the infilling of the Holy Ghost when we repent and accept Christ as our Savior. The second example that reinforces this point is found in Acts 19:1-7. In this example, we see an important question asked by the apostle Paul. This is what it says:

> And it came to pass, that, while Apollos was at Corinth, Paul having passed through the upper coasts came to Ephesus: and finding certain disciples,
>
> He said unto them, Have ye received the Holy Ghost since ye believed? And they said unto him, We have not so much as heard whether there be any Holy Ghost.
>
> And he said unto them, Unto what then were ye baptized? And they said, Unto John's baptism.
>
> Then said Paul, John verily baptized with the baptism of repentance, saying unto the people, that they should believe on him which should come after him, that is, on Christ Jesus.
>
> When they heard this, they were baptized in the name of the Lord Jesus.
>
> And when Paul had laid his hands upon them, the Holy Ghost came on them; and they spake with tongues, and prophesied.
>
> And all the men were about twelve.

Now, let's examine the facts. These twelve men are referred to as disciples. When the apostle Paul encountered them, he acknowledged that he recognized them as fellow believers. There was no dispute from him about their acceptance of Jesus Christ or their faithfulness to God.

In fact, Paul was so certain of their faithfulness to Christ that he inquired about their baptism with a sense of certainty that they had already been baptized. His instincts were correct. They, indeed, had been baptized. So, if Paul recognized them as baptized fellow believers who clearly had accepted Jesus Christ, why did he ask if they had received the Holy Ghost?

Paul asked the question because of his own personal experience. He understood that even though these twelve men had accepted Jesus as Lord, there was a possibility that they might not have received God's Spirit. He was absolutely right. They had not received the Holy Ghost, nor had they even heard of the Holy Ghost. However, based on what they knew at the time, they were following Jesus as their Savior to the best of their ability. They simply had not yet been taught the whole truth about God's plan of salvation.

In Acts 8:5-24, a third passage of Scripture makes this point in an equally compelling manner. This is what it says:

> *Then Philip went down to the city of Samaria, and preached Christ unto them.*
>
> *And the people with one accord gave heed unto those things which Philip spake, hearing and seeing the miracles which he did.*
>
> *For unclean spirits, crying with loud voice, came out of many that were possessed with them: and many taken with palsies, and that were lame, were healed.*
>
> *And there was great joy in that city.*
>
> *But there was a certain man, called Simon, which beforetime in the same city used sorcery, and bewitched the people of Samaria, giving out that himself was some great one:*
>
> *To whom they all gave heed, from the least to the greatest, saying, This man is the great power of God.*
>
> *And to him they had regard, because that of long time he had bewitched them with sorceries.*

But when they believed Philip preaching the things concerning the kingdom of God, and the name of Jesus Christ, they were baptized, both men and women.

Then Simon himself believed also: and when he was baptized, he continued with Philip, and wondered, beholding the miracles and signs which were done.

Now when the apostles which were at Jerusalem heard that Samaria had received the word of God, they sent unto them Peter and John:

Who, when they were come down, prayed for them, that they might receive the Holy Ghost:

(For as yet he was fallen upon none of them: only they were baptized in the name of the Lord Jesus.)

Then laid they their hands on them, and they received the Holy Ghost.

And when Simon saw that through laying on of the apostles' hands the Holy Ghost was given, he offered them money,

Saying, Give me also this power, that on whomsoever I lay hands, he may receive the Holy Ghost.

But Peter said unto him, Thy money perish with thee, because thou hast thought that the gift of God may be purchased with money.

Thou hast neither part nor lot in this matter: for thy heart is not right in the sight of God.

Repent therefore of this thy wickedness, and pray God, if perhaps the thought of thine heart may be forgiven thee.

For I perceive that thou art in the gall of bitterness, and in the bond of iniquity.

Then answered Simon, and said, Pray ye to the Lord for me, that none of these things which ye have spoken come upon me.

We see that even after Simon the sorcerer believed and was baptized, he still had not yet received the Holy Ghost. In fact, he was so desperate to receive the Holy Ghost that he offered to pay for someone to lay hands on him so he could receive the baptism of the Spirit.

Additionally, we see that there were others who had believed and been baptized in the name of Jesus Christ for the remission of sins. However, they did not receive the Holy Ghost until Peter and John were sent to them. When Peter and John arrived, they prayed for them to receive God's Spirit and then laid hands on them, after which they received the Holy Ghost.

It is important to understand that we receive the infilling of God's Spirit through the baptism of the Spirit. It is true that the baptism of the Spirit can and occasionally does occur immediately for some people as soon as they accept Jesus Christ as their Savior. However, it certainly does not occur immediately for everyone.

Fable: The disciples received the Holy Ghost when Jesus breathed on them.

There is an event recorded in John 20:21-22 that has led many people to believe that the disciples received the Holy Ghost when Jesus breathed on them. This is what the passage says:

Then said Jesus to them again, Peace be unto you: as my Father hath sent me, even so send I you.

And when he had said this, he breathed on them, and saith unto them, Receive ye the Holy Ghost:

In addition to teaching that the disciples received the Holy Ghost when Jesus breathed on them, people often use this passage to support the fable that we automatically receive God's Spirit. Some people teach that Jesus "breathes" on us as soon as we confess Him as our Savior, and that is how we immediately receive His Spirit.

First, we have already established that we do not automatically receive the Holy Ghost when we confess Christ as our Savior. The question we must answer, then, is whether the disciples actually received the Holy Ghost when Jesus breathed on them. Let's examine the Word to gain an understanding of what Jesus taught His disciples about how, when, and where they would receive the Holy Ghost. Then, let's examine what actually occurred in this particular incident.

John 13-16 records a lengthy conversation Jesus had with His disciples before He was crucified. During this conversation, He prepared them for many events that would occur soon thereafter, including His departure. He spoke in detail of the coming of the Holy Ghost whom He promised God would send to them as a Comforter. We see this in John 14:16-18 which says:

> *And I will pray the Father, and he shall give you another Comforter, that he may abide with you for ever;*
>
> *Even the Spirit of truth; whom the world cannot receive, because it seeth him not, neither knoweth him: but ye know him; for he dwelleth with you, and shall be in you.*
>
> *I will not leave you comfortless: I will come to you.*

Later, in the same conversation, Jesus makes it clear in John 16:7-13 that He must depart because the Holy Ghost will not come to them until after His departure. This is what He says:

> *Nevertheless I tell you the truth; It is expedient for you that I go away: for if I go not away, the Comforter will not come unto you; but if I depart, I will send him unto you.*

And when he is come, he will reprove the world of sin, and of righteousness, and of judgment:

Of sin, because they believe not on me;

Of righteousness, because I go to my Father, and ye see me no more;

Of judgment, because the prince of this world is judged.

I have yet many things to say unto you, but ye cannot bear them now.

Howbeit when he, the Spirit of truth, is come, he will guide you into all truth: for he shall not speak of himself; but whatsoever he shall hear, that shall he speak: and he will shew you things to come.

After His resurrection, Jesus appeared to His disciples, breathed on them, and told them to receive the Holy Ghost. Later, however, in Acts 1:4-8, Jesus again details how, when, and where they should expect to receive the Holy Ghost. He also explains that they will receive power after receiving the baptism of the Spirit. This is what the passage says:

And, being assembled together with them, [Jesus] commanded them that they should not depart from Jerusalem, but wait for the promise of the Father, which, saith he, ye have heard of me.

For John truly baptized with water; but ye shall be baptized with the Holy Ghost not many days hence.

When they therefore were come together, they asked of him, saying, Lord, wilt thou at this time restore again the kingdom to Israel?

And he said unto them, It is not for you to know the times or the seasons, which the Father hath put in his own power.

> *But ye shall receive power, after that the Holy Ghost is come upon you: and ye shall be witnesses unto me both in Jerusalem, and in all Judaea, and in Samaria, and unto the uttermost part of the earth.*

When Jesus finished speaking, Acts 1:9-11 tells us what happened:

> *And when he had spoken these things, while they beheld, he was taken up; and a cloud received him out of their sight.*

> *And while they looked stedfastly toward heaven as he went up, behold, two men stood by them in white apparel;*

> *Which also said, Ye men of Galilee, why stand ye gazing up into heaven? this same Jesus, which is taken up from you into heaven, shall so come in like manner as ye have seen him go into heaven.*

Pentecost arrived soon thereafter and, just as Jesus promised, they received the Holy Ghost through the baptism of the Spirit – after His departure.

When Jesus breathed on His disciples in John 20, His action was only symbolic of the coming wind of the Spirit that would breathe on them and fill them with the Holy Ghost at Pentecost. The disciples knew they did not receive the Holy Ghost when Jesus breathed on them because He had already told them that the Holy Ghost would not be sent to them until after His departure.

Fable: I already have God's Spirit, but His power will be activated in me later when I receive the baptism of the Spirit.

People who are told that they have received God's Spirit are also often told that the power they received will be activated later when they receive the baptism of the Spirit. It sounds logical to them because there are several examples in the Bible of individuals who have God's Spirit later being anointed with power.

We see an example of this in Acts 4:8 when Peter was "filled" again with the Holy Ghost and anointed with power, enabling him to speak with great boldness against religious leaders who were persecuting the Church. It is important to recognize, however, that Peter had already received the baptism of the Spirit.

As we have already established, we do not have God's Spirit until we receive the baptism of the Spirit. Since it is God's Spirit that gives us His power, there is no power in us to be activated until we receive His Spirit. It is true, however, that after we receive the baptism of the Spirit, the Holy Ghost will frequently come upon us to anoint us with power and enable us to exercise our natural or spiritual gifts at a level that far surpasses our natural abilities.

Fable: There is no evidence to help us determine who has received the baptism of the Spirit.

When we are baptized in the name of Jesus Christ for the remission of sins and we emerge from the water dripping wet from head to toe, we have a reasonable assurance that we received a proper water baptism. We are confident in our baptism because we have evidence that it occurred. The water is our evidence.

However, unlike water, God's Spirit is invisible and intangible. Since being born of the Spirit is required for our salvation, surely we would expect God to give us some concrete evidence to confirm when we have received the baptism of the Spirit.

Fortunately, the Bible provides a well documented trail pointing to the evidence that demonstrates that the baptism of the Spirit has occurred.

Let's begin in the New Testament by examining what Jesus said in Mark 16:15-18 when He explains how to determine who has received the baptism:

> *And he said unto them, Go ye into all the world, and preach the gospel to every creature.*
>
> *He that believeth and is baptized shall be saved; but he that believeth not shall be damned.*

And these signs shall follow them that believe; In my name shall they cast out devils; they shall speak with new tongues;

They shall take up serpents; and if they drink any deadly thing, it shall not hurt them; they shall lay hands on the sick, and they shall recover.

Jesus told the apostles what evidence to look for in those who have believed and been baptized. Then, as we noted previously, He instructed them in Acts 1 to wait in Jerusalem and pray until they received the baptism of the Spirit.

Later, in Acts 2, when the day of Pentecost arrived, God poured out His Spirit. Those who received the baptism of the Spirit spoke in tongues, and miracles, signs, and wonders followed as Jesus promised.

When we receive the baptism of the Spirit, God gives us an accompanying gift of a heavenly prayer language that enables us to speak in tongues. That is the first evidence that confirms that the baptism of the Spirit has occurred.

We first see it in Acts 2 on Pentecost. Later, in Acts 10, we see the same thing occur during Peter's visit to Cornelius. Peter and those who traveled with him to visit Cornelius were able to confirm that Cornelius and his entire household had received the baptism of the Spirit when they heard them speak in tongues. Acts 10:44-48 says:

While Peter yet spake these words, the Holy Ghost fell on all them which heard the word.

And they of the circumcision which believed were astonished, as many as came with Peter, because that on the Gentiles also was poured out the gift of the Holy Ghost.

For they heard them speak with tongues, and magnify God. Then answered Peter,

Can any man forbid water, that these should not be baptized, which have received the Holy Ghost as well as we?

And he commanded them to be baptized in the name of the Lord. Then prayed they him to tarry certain days.

In Acts 19:1-7, we examined another example that illustrates the evidence of the baptism of the Spirit. It is the example of the disciples Paul encountered who had accepted Jesus, but had not yet received the Holy Ghost. After Paul baptized them in the name of Jesus Christ and laid hands on them, they, too, received the Holy Ghost and spoke in tongues.

Jesus explained how to determine who has received the baptism. Then, once the apostles personally experienced it at Pentecost, they knew what to look for to determine when others had received it. Nothing has changed from Pentecost to today. Speaking in tongues is still the first evidence we find when the baptism of the Spirit has occurred. In addition to the explanation Jesus provided, there are other Scriptures that are also helpful to reference.

For example, when the outpouring of God's Spirit occurred on Pentecost, many mockers laughed and ridiculed what they observed. They presumed that those who had received the baptism of the Spirit were drunk.

However, Peter invited them to compare their beliefs to the prophecy foretelling the arrival of God's Spirit recorded in Joel 2:28-32. While Peter's sermon only refers us back to what is written by Joel, Joel is not the only prophet in the Old Testament who speaks of the outpouring of the Holy Spirit.

Isaiah 28:9-13 foretells of God speaking to His people through stammering lips and another tongue. It says:

Whom shall he teach knowledge? and whom shall he make to understand doctrine? them that are weaned from the milk, and drawn from the breasts.

For precept must be upon precept, precept upon precept; line upon line, line upon line; here a little, and there a little:

For with stammering lips and another tongue will he speak to this people.

To whom he said, This is the rest wherewith ye may cause the weary to rest; and this is the refreshing: yet they would not hear.

But the word of the LORD was unto them precept upon precept, precept upon precept; line upon line, line upon line; here a little, and there a little; that they might go, and fall backward, and be broken, and snared, and taken.

God gives us a great deal of information about the baptism of the Spirit in this passage. When we receive the baptism of the Spirit, it causes the weary to rest and God's Spirit refreshes us. Sadly, however, many people miss the instruction and understanding God gives us in His Word because it is not neatly packaged all in one place

If we desire to know the truth, we must diligently search the Bible to find it. Those who fail to do so will "fall backward, and be broken, snared, and taken."

We see that same message again in 1 Corinthians 14:21-22 which says:

In the law it is written, With men of other tongues and other lips will I speak unto this people; and yet for all that will they not hear me, saith the Lord.

Wherefore tongues are for a sign, not to them that believe, but to them that believe not: but prophesying serveth not for them that believe not, but for them which believe.

It is foretold in the Old Testament. It is demonstrated in the New Testament. Yet, even if we miss what is written in all of the other supporting Scriptures, we can still rely on what Jesus said. Jesus said that those who believe will speak in tongues. He proved it on Pentecost, He proved it in multiple examples recorded in Acts, and He still proves it today each time

He baptizes someone with His Spirit. Speaking in tongues will always be the initial evidence to look for to confirm that the baptism of the Spirit has occurred.

Fable: Speaking in tongues isn't for everyone. It's a gift God only gives to some people.

From the early Church to today, many religious leaders have dismissed the importance of speaking in tongues. Many refuse to acknowledge it as the evidence of the baptism of the Spirit. Some people believe that speaking in tongues was only for the early Church and that it is not a gift that is available to us today.

Others acknowledge the gift as one that is available to today's believers. Unfortunately, many people often read about spiritual gifts in 1 Corinthians 12, 13 and 14 and conclude that speaking in tongues is a gift that is not for everyone. The Bible tells us, however, in 1 Corinthians 12:10 that there are "divers kinds of tongues," as well as the gift of the interpretation of tongues.

As we examine three types of tongues recorded in the Bible along with some supporting Scriptures, I believe it will become evident that one of those gifts of tongues is, in fact, for everyone.

The first gift of tongues, the gift of a known tongue, is demonstrated in Acts 2:1-12 which says:

> *And when the day of Pentecost was fully come, they were all with one accord in one place.*
>
> *And suddenly there came a sound from heaven as of a rushing mighty wind, and it filled all the house where they were sitting.*
>
> *And there appeared unto them cloven tongues like as of fire, and it sat upon each of them.*
>
> *And they were all filled with the Holy Ghost, and began to speak with other tongues, as the Spirit gave them utterance.*

And there were dwelling at Jerusalem Jews, devout men, out of every nation under heaven.

Now when this was noised abroad, the multitude came together, and were confounded, because that every man heard them speak in his own language.

And they were all amazed and marvelled, saying one to another, Behold, are not all these which speak Galilaeans?

And how hear we every man in our own tongue, wherein we were born?

Parthians, and Medes, and Elamites, and the dwellers in Mesopotamia, and in Judaea, and Cappadocia, in Pontus, and Asia,

Phrygia, and Pamphylia, in Egypt, and in the parts of Libya about Cyrene, and strangers of Rome, Jews and proselytes,

Cretes and Arabians, we do hear them speak in our tongues the wonderful works of God.

And they were all amazed, and were in doubt, saying one to another, What meaneth this?

As we see from this passage, the gift of a known tongue is demonstrated when someone speaks a language that is unknown to the speaker. However, it is a common language that is known and understood by those who are listening.

For example, God may use someone whose native language is French to speak on His behalf in Spanish to a person whose native language is Spanish. The person who speaks French does not know Spanish, yet God anoints that individual at that particular time to speak Spanish.

Even at the moment that individual is being used by God to speak Spanish, he or she may have no knowledge of what is being said. However, the person who understands Spanish will clearly understand what is being said.

This particular gift of tongues is not one that we can use at our own discretion or call upon at any given time. It is a gift that is available when God anoints an individual to meet a particular need.

Interestingly, the gift of a known tongue reverses the effects of what God did in Genesis to impede our ability to communicate freely with one another. We see that story in Genesis 11:1-9:

> *And the whole earth was of one language, and of one speech.*
>
> *And it came to pass, as they journeyed from the east, that they found a plain in the land of Shinar; and they dwelt there.*
>
> *And they said one to another, Go to, let us make brick, and burn them thoroughly. And they had brick for stone, and slime had they for morter.*
>
> *And they said, Go to, let us build us a city and a tower, whose top may reach unto heaven; and let us make us a name, lest we be scattered abroad upon the face of the whole earth.*
>
> *And the LORD came down to see the city and the tower, which the children of men builded.*
>
> *And the LORD said, Behold, the people is one, and they have all one language; and this they begin to do: and now nothing will be restrained from them, which they have imagined to do.*
>
> *Go to, let us go down, and there confound their language, that they may not understand one another's speech.*

So the LORD scattered them abroad from thence upon the face of all the earth: and they left off to build the city.

Therefore is the name of it called Babel; because the LORD did there confound the language of all the earth: and from thence did the LORD scatter them abroad upon the face of all the earth.

Clearly, God controls how language is used. When man attempted to use language to strive against God, He supernaturally intervened and confused our ability to communicate.

However, when He needed to use people who spoke in different languages to communicate on His behalf on Pentecost, He again intervened supernaturally. This time He enabled people to speak the language of His choosing under His anointing and direction. God creates and transcends language barriers to hinder or facilitate communication whenever He chooses to do so.

The second gift of tongues, the gift of an unknown tongue, is addressed in 1 Corinthians 14:2 which says:

For he that speaketh in an unknown tongue speaketh not unto men, but unto God: for no man understandeth him; howbeit in the spirit he speaketh mysteries.

The purpose of this gift is for man to speak to God on behalf of the body of Christ. However, what is being spoken is not understood by those present unless the individual speaking, or another person present, has the gift of interpreting tongues. Only then can what is spoken be translated or interpreted for the benefit of those present.

The gift of a known tongue and the gift of an unknown tongue are gifts we are to use to benefit the body of Christ. The third gift of tongues, however, is not given to us to benefit the body of Christ. It is a gift given to each of us individually when we receive the baptism of the Holy Ghost. This is the gift that is referenced in Acts 2:38 which says:

Then Peter said unto them, Repent, and be baptized every one of you in the name of Jesus Christ for the remission of sins, and ye shall receive the gift of the Holy Ghost.

Acts 2:38 refers to it as "the gift of the Holy Ghost." Peter tells us that this gift is one that God promised to us. It is our assurance that we have received the baptism of the Spirit.

The Bible does not say God *might* give us the gift. It says God *promises* to give it to us, to our children, and to all whom He has called. If God has called you, then He has promised to give you the gift of the Holy Ghost and you should expect to receive it.

Fable: Speaking in tongues is just senseless babbling.

Many people find it unbelievable that God has given His people a unique language to communicate with Him, but that should not come as a surprise to us. We have already examined God's history of supernaturally intervening in our communication.

When we enter into the kingdom of God, we must understand that we have become citizens of a real kingdom and a real nation – a holy nation. We see that in 1 Peter 2:9-10 which says:

But ye are a chosen generation, a royal priesthood, an holy nation, a peculiar people; that ye should shew forth the praises of him who hath called you out of darkness into his marvellous light;

Which in time past were not a people, but are now the people of God: which had not obtained mercy, but now have obtained mercy.

In the natural realm we recognize that people from different nations have their own unique languages. French. English. Hebrew. Swahili. Japanese. Spanish. Chinese. All sound unique, yet all effectively facilitate communication.

When we become citizens of the kingdom of God, we receive the native language of our new land. Just as we communicate with our natural fathers in our natural language, we speak in tongues to communicate with our heavenly Father in His language.

We use our natural languages to articulate the thoughts of the rational, natural mind of man. Conversely, we use our spiritual language to transcend the limitations of the natural mind and access the mind of Christ.

Fable: I understand that I need to pray, but praying in tongues is not an essential part of the Christian experience.

People often dismiss the importance of speaking in tongues after receiving the gift of the Holy Ghost because they do not understand its purpose or its power. However, speaking in tongues is absolutely an essential part of the Christian experience.

Our prayer language is given to us by God to activate His Spirit to intercede on our behalf. This is how Romans 8:26-27 explains it:

> *Likewise the Spirit also helpeth our infirmities: for we know not what we should pray for as we ought: but the Spirit itself maketh intercession for us with groanings which cannot be uttered.*
>
> *And he that searcheth the hearts knoweth what is the mind of the Spirit, because he maketh intercession for the saints according to the will of God.*

There are times in all of our lives when we do not know how we should pray. In those times of great uncertainty or despair when there is nowhere to turn for answers, the Holy Ghost takes over and prays the perfect prayers on our behalf.

How is that possible?

The Holy Ghost intercedes and prays God's perfect will for us because the Spirit knows all things. This is what Jesus tells us about the Holy Ghost in John 16:13-15:

> *Howbeit when he, the Spirit of truth, is come, he will guide you into all truth: for he shall not speak of himself; but whatsoever he shall hear, that shall he speak: and he will shew you things to come.*

He shall glorify me: for he shall receive of mine, and shall shew it unto you.

All things that the Father hath are mine: therefore said I, that he shall take of mine, and shall shew it unto you.

The Holy Ghost knows the otherwise unsearchable depths of God. He uses His knowledge to intercede on our behalf. He prays about things we could not possibly know to pray for because He has knowledge that we do not have.

Imagine being a newly arrived immigrant in an unfamiliar land. Immigrants who cannot speak the language of their new land are unable to communicate their basic needs. They are unable to receive instruction about basic things that would greatly assist them. They are vulnerable and often fall prey to schemes intended to take advantage of their vulnerabilities.

A well informed translator and advocate, however, can make all the difference in the world for new immigrants. Such an individual may understand the laws of the land, avenues for accessing vital resources, and people and places that should be avoided. A well connected advocate may also know influential people who can open doors of opportunity and give preferential treatment that others would love to receive.

Unless new immigrants can find someone who speaks their language and is willing to translate and advocate on their behalf, it is unlikely that they will survive, thrive, and ultimately prosper in the new land.

When we become citizens of the kingdom of God, we find ourselves in a similar situation. Suddenly, we are brand new citizens in a brand new kingdom, susceptible to the tricks and traps of the devil who seeks to prey upon us and destroy us. I encourage you to seriously consider what the Bible tells us about the devil.

In John 10:10:

> *The thief cometh not, but for to steal, and to kill, and to destroy: I [Jesus] am come that they might have life, and that they might have it more abundantly.*

In 1 Peter 5:8:

> *Be sober, be vigilant; because your adversary the devil, as a roaring lion, walketh about, seeking whom he may devour:*

In 2 Timothy 2:24-26:

> *And the servant of the Lord must not strive; but be gentle unto all men, apt to teach, patient,*
>
> *In meekness instructing those that oppose themselves; if God per-adventure will give them repentance to the acknowledging of the truth;*
>
> *And that they may recover themselves out of the snare of the devil, who are taken captive by him at his will.*

The devil is set on destroying us. He fully intends to keep us from learning the truth about salvation so we will never make it into the kingdom of God.

Even after we become citizens of the kingdom of God we must always remember that we are still in a war for our souls. We must still fight daily to thrive in this world until we get to heaven. We cannot afford to be taken captive by the devil, yet 2 Timothy 2:26 tells us that the devil takes us captive at will. The devil has set tricks, traps, snares, and fables everywhere. We must recognize them and avoid them. When we fall prey to them, we must quickly recognize what has happened and get free.

No responsible father would take his children into a new land where they cannot communicate without providing for their care, nor would God do that to His children. That is why He has given us the Holy Ghost.

The Holy Ghost is our well informed, well connected Advocate who is fluent in the language of the land. Our Advocate will give us all the help we need. When we speak in tongues we, too, are immediately fluent in the language of our new land. When we pray, our Translator and Advocate immediately goes to work on our behalf.

Remember that the Holy Ghost is the Spirit of Christ. When we pray in the Holy Ghost, we have access to all of the wisdom and knowledge in the mind of Jesus Christ who is our Intercessor, our Advocate, and our High Priest.

That is why it is so important for us to understand that God does not give only some of His children the ability to pray in tongues to receive intercession from the Holy Ghost. He would not adopt you, then leave you helpless and defenseless without access to the intercession that you desperately need. He gives all of us the gift of the Holy Ghost when we receive the baptism of the Spirit. It is a tremendously valuable gift that God expects us to use.

No matter how it sounds when we pray in our heavenly language, we must know that it is a language that is absolutely perfect for us. My prayer language is perfect for me. Yours is perfect for you. When you receive the baptism of the Spirit, use your prayer language. It may initially sound and feel peculiar to speak in tongues. Do it anyway. Whether your prayer language sounds like babbling, grunting, groaning, or a beautiful melodic flow is irrelevant. What matters is that the Holy Ghost is interceding for you, God hears those prayers, and He is moving heaven and earth on your behalf.

Fable: If you don't speak in tongues, you're not saved.

I have heard people who have received the baptism of the Spirit tell others that unless a person speaks in tongues, they are not saved. That is not what the Bible says.

Jesus said that we must be born of the Spirit. That is the requirement for entering into the kingdom of God. He also told us what evidence to look for in those who have been born of the Spirit. Speaking in tongues provides evidence that the baptism of the Spirit has occurred.

However, as you will see in the following chapter, many people may have received the baptism of the Spirit without understanding what happened to them. They may have spoken in tongues when they received the baptism of the Spirit. However, they may not have spoken in tongues since that occurrence because they have not been taught the importance of using their prayer language. In fact, they may not even recognize that they have received a prayer language.

God does not necessarily wait until we understand the baptism of the Spirit before He baptizes us. He baptizes us when He is ready to do so.

Our understanding of the baptism experience, however, may not occur until much later.

Additionally, there are other factors that must be taken into consideration when we address speaking in tongues. For example, someone who is mute will not audibly speak in tongues unless God miraculously gives them the ability to speak. That does not mean that they have not received the baptism of the Spirit. Someone who is near death and is so weak that they can no longer speak can still be filled with God's Spirit without audibly speaking in tongues.

Someone who is in a coma may not be able to communicate with us. That does not mean that they cannot communicate with God or that God cannot communicate with them. They, too, can still receive God's Spirit without us ever being aware of what has occurred.

We must remember that God moves outside the boundaries of our understanding. It is impossible for us to define parameters to conclusively determine how or when the baptism of the Spirit has occurred. Therefore, we should not definitively conclude that someone has not received the baptism of the Spirit because we have not personally heard them speak in tongues or because they cannot report that they have spoken in tongues. God can fill anyone with His Spirit whenever He so chooses.

I once had an experience with an elderly man who was in the advanced stages of Alzheimer's disease. He had lost his language skills and was no longer able to communicate intelligibly. He had almost completely lost his memory and his cognitive functioning was greatly impaired.

Nonetheless, one day he was able to make me understand that he could hear the voice of God speaking to him. He was particularly distressed, anxious, and agitated in his spirit that day. However, though he could not speak, he was able to convey to me that he needed me to pray for him.

When I realized what he was sharing with me about his relationship with God and his need for prayer, I told him that I would pray with him. Before we prayed, however, I decided to share a personal prayer request with him. There was something in particular that I wanted him to ask of God for me. I had been praying about that issue for nearly twenty years, but God had not moved on my prayer request. When I shared my prayer request with this man, he indicated that he understood what I wanted and he agreed to pray for it.

Quite frankly, I had no idea whether he really understood me or not. I simply decided to ask him to pray for what I wanted from God, so we prayed together. As soon as we finished praying, I sensed the peace of God come over him and I knew that God had comforted his heart. I am certain, however, that even two minutes after we prayed, he did not remember that we had prayed together nor did he remember my prayer request.

Yet, the following day, I witnessed the most remarkable miracle. God answered that man's prayer for me. In over twenty years, God had not responded to my prayer request. Yet, when an elderly man with Alzheimer's prayed for me, God answered his prayer in one day.

That man was my father. As I ministered to him in the final days of his life, he could not speak at all. He had no vocal ability whatsoever. He could only make eye contact with me and occasionally blink his eyes to acknowledge that he understood me. I know that he was still making peace with God at the end of his life. I personally witnessed what God did for him during that time and I firmly believe that he received the Holy Ghost before he died.

Through my experiences with my father shortly before his death, God taught me in a deeply personal way how He honors the prayers of the heart. My father was a feeble, dying man in a nursing care facility who desperately needed Jesus. He could no longer read, go to church, or hold an intelligent conversation with anyone about the requirements of salvation. He was a lost sheep who was as helpless as a baby. He could not go looking for Jesus. Yet, something in his heart must have cried out to Jesus, so Jesus came looking for him.

1 Timothy 2:3-6 says this:

> *For this is good and acceptable in the sight of God our Saviour;*

> *Who will have all men to be saved, and to come unto the knowledge of the truth.*

> *For there is one God, and one mediator between God and men, the man Christ Jesus;*

> *Who gave himself a ransom for all, to be testified in due time.*

Jesus Christ is the Good Shepherd who died and rose again for a purpose. He did it to save lost sheep. Jesus did not die to save only those who have been taught about the Holy Ghost. He did not die to save only those who are strong enough to speak aloud in tongues. He did not die to save only those whose minds are sound enough to understand the requirements of salvation so they can make a well informed decision about their faith.

This is what Jesus said in John 10:27-29:

My sheep hear my voice, and I know them, and they follow me:

And I give unto them eternal life; and they shall never perish, neither shall any man pluck them out of my hand.

My Father, which gave them me, is greater than all; and no man is able to pluck them out of my Father's hand.

There is nothing more important to Jesus than saving His sheep. We must recognize that He continually works outside the boundaries of our understanding to accomplish that purpose. The evidence of speaking in tongues gives us proof that we have received the Spirit of Christ. Jesus, however, does not need to hear us speak in tongues to confirm for Himself that we have been baptized with His Spirit. That is why we must be careful not to perpetuate the fable that it is impossible for someone to have received the baptism of the Spirit if they have not audibly spoken in tongues. The Bible tells us in Luke 1:37 that nothing is impossible with God.

My father was a man who could no longer speak, yet he was a sheep who could still hear and follow the Shepherd's voice. I believe that God saved him. We must have faith that God will give His Spirit to anyone with a pure heart, though we may never hear them speak

CHAPTER 10

The Baptism Experience

Just as God gives each of us a uniquely different prayer language, He also gives us uniquely different experiences when we receive the baptism of the Spirit. That is why it is important to share examples of different people's experiences.

For many people, the baptism of the Spirit is an unforgettable, overwhelmingly emotional experience. They may have an experience that is physically and vocally demonstrative like the baptism of the Spirit experience described on Pentecost in Acts 2.

They may find themselves on the floor weeping and praying in tongues for hours, losing all sense of time and space. Their baptism might occur in a public setting such as at church, or it may occur in the privacy of their home. Wherever it happens, these individuals will more than likely remember the date, time, place, and specific details of their baptism experience.

That is not the case for everyone. Many people have a quiet, relatively uneventful baptism experience. My daughter, for example, as a young teen, was filled with the Spirit while sitting alone in her bedroom one night.

She had just watched the movie The Passion of the Christ and she was deeply grieved about the horrific suffering Jesus experienced to save us.

When the movie ended, she went to her room, got on her knees, and began to fervently pray. Within a few minutes, she suddenly began speaking in tongues. She had no idea what had occurred and she never mentioned the incident to me.

A few weeks later, she and I were discussing the importance of receiving the baptism of the Spirit. I wanted her to understand why I had been encouraging her to go to the altar at church for prayer.

Each time I had encouraged her to go, she refused. She insisted that she was not ready to receive the baptism of the Spirit, but she never explained why. Her attitude puzzled me. In fact, it irritated me. I just could not understand why she was reluctant to receive God's Spirit. I believed that she was being hard-hearted, rebellious, and resistant to God. I was wrong.

That evening as we talked, I discovered something that surprised me. My daughter truly did want to receive the baptism of the Spirit. However, she believed that she was not emotionally ready for the experience. She was afraid that what she had seen happen to others would happen to her, too.

She believed that she would have a wild experience in which her body would be taken over by the Spirit of God. She was afraid that she would lose control, become loud and demonstrative, shouting and falling on the floor. That is what she had observed with others who had been filled with the Holy Ghost. She assumed that is what happens to everyone and she certainly did not want it to happen to her.

As a young teen, the thought of losing control of herself and being overtaken by the Holy Ghost was horrifying. It was particularly unsettling to think that it would happen in front of the whole church. So, as much as she wanted to receive God's Spirit, she refused to go to the altar. Instead, she sat in church each week trying to prepare mentally and emotionally for the experience.

When I began to explain to her what occurs when we receive the baptism of the Spirit, we made the surprising discovery that she had received the baptism of the Spirit weeks earlier. She was so excited to know that what she had been waiting for was already done. God did not baptize her through some horrifying experience that left her lying on the floor in front of the entire church. He quietly baptized her in the privacy of her bedroom.

Once we realized that she had received the baptism of the Spirit, I began to teach her about the importance of praying in tongues. I learned, however, that she was not comfortable praying in tongues in front of me or anyone else. I simply continued to pray with her as we always had, and I encouraged her to pray in tongues during her private time with God.

Soon thereafter, I began to recognize how Jesus was healing my daughter's heart and changing her life. She was becoming a brand new person right before my eyes. She began to open her heart and allow people to help her deal with the issues of her life. She could sense God speaking to her, correcting her behavior, and guiding her thoughts and decisions. She was becoming more pleasant and more obedient. She began to sincerely repent and apologize when she knew she was wrong. I often sensed deep remorse in her heart when she failed in her behavior. After each failure, she was determined to try harder and to do better.

I was amazed at how quickly Jesus was healing the broken places in her heart and her life. Slowly but surely, He was setting her free. As He did, she became more mentally and emotionally available to become the person God created her to be. Her self-esteem, attitude, and behavior improved. Her relationships improved. Her grades improved. Her entire life changed. She could hardly wait to get to church. She fell in love with praise and worship. She was eager to hear good teaching and preaching. She learned to genuinely enjoy being around people whose lives reflected the love of Christ.

My daughter was no longer a teenager who hated school, shunned people, found little joy in life, and had no clear sense of direction for her future. She was a beautiful, vibrant young woman with a bright future and an absolute passion for life. Most of all, she was excited about discovering and pursuing the wonderful plans she was certain God had created just for her.

God was able to heal my daughter's heart and change her life because I taught her the truth I had learned. She placed her faith in Jesus Christ and repented for her sins. Repentance has remained an ongoing part of her life. She chose to be baptized in the name of Jesus Christ for the remission of her sins. Soon thereafter, God filled her with His Spirit, drew her in, and healed her heart. The Word of God became the standard by which she allowed God to set boundaries for her life. God used His Word and His Spirit to lead her into obedience when I could not. During difficult times, her faith in God encouraged her to hold onto hope until God's promises were manifested in her life.

Parenting is hard work. Parenting children who have challenging issues of their own is *incredibly* hard work. However, through that experience, I learned that life gets progressively easier for us and for our children when we all have the Holy Ghost. Life gets easier because Jesus steps in to help with the work of parenting. He helps by healing the broken places in our children's hearts that they cannot heal for themselves and we cannot heal for them. He also helps us to have patience with them along the way. That is why Acts 2:38-39 tells us that God's promise of the gift of the Holy Ghost is for us *and* for our children.

When we fully embrace that truth, we will begin to understand that too often we expect our children to do things they are not spiritually, emotionally, or mentally capable of doing. Until we receive the Spirit of Christ, we cannot be Christ-like. The same is true of our children.

Jesus knew that my daughter needed the Holy Ghost and He knew when she was ready. I didn't need to push her to go to the altar. I just needed to pray for her. God handled the rest all by Himself in the privacy of her bedroom when He quietly baptized her with His Spirit.

In another situation, I discovered that a friend of mine had also received the baptism of the Spirit. Like my daughter, she did not understand what had happened to her. Our discovery came during a conversation when I shared with her what it means to be born of the Spirit. I also explained about the evidence of speaking in tongues.

My friend said that she does not speak in tongues, but she was certain that she has God's Spirit. I was resistant and insisted that if she truly has God's Spirit, she would also have spoken in tongues. She disagreed. Not only did she disagree, she was deeply offended by the suggestion that perhaps she did not yet have God's Spirit.

As the conversation progressed and I shared more with her about the baptism experience, she remembered that she had actually spoken in tongues once. She said God gave her just one short phrase that she clearly remembered.

In fact, she had written it down many years earlier so she would always remember it and she shared it with me.

She had no idea what it was at the time that she first spoke it. She did not know what it meant or why she continued to repeat it, yet she seemed to have a sense that it was something that had come from God. She did not, however, continue to pray in that manner after her initial experience.

I told her that I believe God has filled her with His Spirit and He has given her a prayer language. She has the ability to speak in tongues. She simply had no idea what occurred when she received the baptism of the Spirit. She did not continue to speak in tongues because she had not been taught about the purpose or the power of her gift.

Only later did I realize why my friend was so reluctant to receive the truth that I was trying to share with her. Both of her parents were deceased and she was fairly certain that neither of them had ever spoken in tongues. My friend described her mother as a deeply faithful woman who truly loved God. She refused to believe that it was possible that God had rejected her mother because she did not speak in tongues.

I realized that in sharing with her about the baptism of the Spirit, I had focused more on speaking in tongues than on the total baptism experience. That is when I learned how it important it is for us to be careful about how we communicate the truth.

If my friend had not already received the baptism of the Spirit, she might have refused to hear what I had to say. Her fear was that I wanted her to believe it was impossible that God had saved her deceased loved ones because they did not speak in tongues.

We must give people a realistic sense of hope that God may have saved their loved ones even though they may never have heard their loved ones speak in tongues. When we give people that sense of hope, they will be more likely to hear the truth about receiving the baptism of the Spirit as a requirement for their own salvation. Additionally, they will be more likely to share that truth with others.

People often ask me to share my experience with receiving the Holy Ghost. I wish that I could, but I cannot. My daughter and my friend both remember their baptism experiences, though they did not understand what happened to them.

I, on the other hand, have no recollection of when I received the baptism of the Spirit. I cannot remember when I began speaking in tongues. I only know that I have God's Spirit and I have spoken in tongues for many years. However, I did not begin to exercise consistent use of my prayer language until I learned about its value many years later.

Clearly, there are people who have not received the baptism of the Spirit who believe that they have. Conversely, there are people who have received God's Spirit who do not know that they have the Holy Ghost. That is why it is so important for both types of individuals to receive proper teaching on what it means to receive the baptism of the Spirit.

Further, it is imperative that we learn to ask the right probing questions to discern whether someone actually has the Holy Ghost. We must be able to help those who do not have the Holy Ghost understand that they need to receive the baptism of the Spirit. We must also be able to help those who do have the Holy Ghost learn how to use the precious gift that God has given them. Now let's examine some more examples of baptism experiences.

There are people who repent and accept Jesus Christ as their Lord and Savior. They immediately get baptized and, as soon as they emerge from the water, they are speaking in tongues.

Then there are examples like those that we have previously examined. We saw what occurred with the disciples that Paul encountered in Ephesus in Acts 19:1-7. We also saw the example of the believers that Peter and John encountered in Acts 8:14-17.

The disciples with Paul had never heard of the Holy Ghost, while those with Peter and John had heard, but they had not yet received the baptism of the Spirit. They had done all that they could do by accepting Jesus Christ and getting baptized in the name of Jesus. However, they simply had to wait patiently on God's appointed time for them to receive the baptism of the Spirit. All eventually received the baptism of the Spirit when the apostles laid hands on them and prayed for them.

Many people have to work much harder to receive the Holy Ghost. Some people have to labor intensely in prayer for hours with the assistance of others who pray fervently along with them before they receive the gift. Sometimes it takes praying together on multiple occasions before they finally receive the baptism of the Spirit. This is not uncommon. Matthew 18:19-20 tells us that there is power in praying together with two or three people. Fervent prayer to receive the baptism of the Spirit is often referred to as "tarrying for the Holy Ghost." Some churches hold tarrying services for people to come specifically to pray to receive the baptism of the Spirit. Those services are not as common as they once were, but some churches do offer them on occasion.

I also know of people who have prayed for many years before being filled with the Spirit. Simon the sorcerer whose story we read in Acts 8 may have been such an individual. The Bible says he was so eager to receive the baptism of the Spirit that he was willing to pay for it, but he did not receive it when he asked for it.

We learn so much about the Holy Ghost through people's testimonies of their baptism of the Spirit experience. One of my favorite stories came from a delightful blind woman I met who had just been baptized in the name of Jesus and filled with the Holy Ghost. I do not know her age, but she had an adult daughter in her thirties. Despite her age and obvious maturity, she had a childlike joy and enthusiasm about being filled with the Holy Ghost. She shared that one day not long after her water baptism, she was sitting at home with her cat on her lap singing to the Lord. Suddenly, she began singing in tongues and she knew God had filled her with the Holy Ghost. She got so excited that she immediately began sharing her testimony with some of her blind friends. Two of them got baptized right away and received the Holy Ghost.

The baptism of the Spirit truly transcends every physical and religious boundary. The Lord reminded me of that when a dear friend who is Catholic called me one day absolutely giddy with excitement because God made her a believer in the gift of the Holy Ghost. While driving to work one morning, she spontaneously began praying for nearly ten minutes in a language that sounded like Hebrew. I witnessed another Catholic acquaintance ask for prayer to receive the baptism of the Spirit while attending a Christian women's conference. When someone laid hands on her and prayed, she spoke in tongues within a matter of minutes.

Unfortunately, many of us have preconceived ideas about religions and denominations. Many Catholics, for example, believe the biblical requirements for becoming a born again believer are unique to Protestants. Yet, Acts 1:14 tells us that even the Virgin Mary was among the baptized believers Jesus told to remain in Jerusalem and wait to be filled with the Holy Ghost. Mary's presence among those believers strongly suggests that she, too, was baptized in the name of Jesus Christ and filled with the Holy Ghost with the evidence of speaking in tongues.

It is easy for any of us to err when we focus on religious traditions and lose sight of the Word of God. Jesus did not establish religious institutions. He established sound biblical doctrine. Thankfully, God looks beyond religious institutions and baptizes us individually with His Spirit.

If you have not yet received the baptism of the Spirit, God will fill you when you are truly ready. He knows you personally and intimately and He will give you the perfect baptism experience. Just ask God for His Spirit, relax, and begin to pray. Lift your hands toward heaven as you pray and thank Jesus for all that He has done for you. Offer praises to God. Lift your voice and say "Hallelujah! Thank you, Jesus!" Trust God to lead you in prayer. Worship Him in song and cry out to Him with a hunger in your heart.

If you do not receive the baptism of the Spirit the first time you pray, continue to persevere. If you have done all that you know to do, I encourage you to do some deep soul searching. Carefully examine your walk with God. Acts 5:31-32 tells us that God will give His Spirit to people who obey Him. Ask Him to help you identify what is keeping you from receiving it. He will show you in a manner that you will understand. When He does, repent, ask Him to help you overcome those issues, then make a sincere effort to change.

Baptism could be the key to your ability to receive the Holy Ghost. Read Acts 19:1-7 again. When Paul encountered the twelve believers who had not yet been properly baptized, he baptized them again in the name of Jesus Christ, laid hands on them, and they immediately received the Holy Ghost.

Are there people in your life you have not forgiven? Are there people you have hurt? Apologize and ask for their forgiveness. Continue to search your heart, pray, and seek God. If you still do not receive the baptism of the Spirit, have someone pray with you. If there is no one among your friends or in your church who is Spirit-filled and knows how to pray with you, contact a local church. Many churches have people who can and will pray with you. Commit to doing whatever is necessary to receive the baptism of the Spirit. When you search for God with all your heart, you will find Him and He will fill you with His Spirit.

When He does, thank Him for the blessing, then use your prayer language with consistency! Most of all, remember that when God fills you with the Holy Ghost, He has filled you with something *holy*. He has filled you with Himself and made you a holy vessel and a temple of the living God. Therefore, you should expect Him to separate you from everything unholy, including people, places, thoughts and beliefs, and things. This is especially true of churches, religions, and religious leaders as we see in 2 Corinthians 6:14-18 which says:

> *Be ye not unequally yoked together with unbelievers: for what fellowship hath righteousness with unrighteousness? and what communion hath light with darkness?*

> *And what concord hath Christ with Belial? or what part hath he that believeth with an infidel?*

> *And what agreement hath the temple of God with idols? for ye are the temple of the living God; as God hath said, I will dwell in them, and walk in them; and I will be their God, and they shall be my people.*

> *Wherefore come out from among them, and be ye separate, saith the Lord, and touch not the unclean thing; and I will receive you.*

> *And will be a Father unto you, and ye shall be my sons and daughters, saith the Lord Almighty.*

God gives us His Spirit and makes us His sons and daughters so He can lead us. He leads us out of darkness, away from religions founded on the traditions of men, and into truth, light, and holiness. In fact, this is what Jesus says in Mark 7:6-9 when rebuking religious leaders who challenge why His disciples do not follow their religious traditions:

He answered and said unto them, Well hath Esaias prophesied of you hypocrites, as it is written, This people honoureth me with their lips, but their heart is far from me.

Howbeit in vain do they worship me, teaching for doctrines the commandments of men.

For laying aside the commandment of God, ye hold the tradition of men, as the washing of pots and cups: and many other such like things ye do.

And he said unto them, Full well ye reject the commandment of God, that ye may keep your own tradition.

Remember this simple truth. There are only two kingdoms. There are only two groups. There are only two leaders, both of whom unquestionably lead their followers on a road to an eternal destiny. By His Spirit, Jesus leads sheep to heaven.

You must know that, regardless of what any religious leader says, a religious leader who rejects what Jesus Christ teaches has rejected Jesus Christ. That individual is not on the road you want to travel and they are not being led by the spirit you want to follow. Make certain that you are in a church that is led by the Holy Ghost. If you are in a religion or church that does not teach sound biblical doctrine, the Spirit of God will lead the leader to change the doctrine or He will lead you out of darkness and into a new place.

If you find it difficult to follow God's leading to separate yourself from a religion, rituals, traditions, or religious leaders, it is likely because you are struggling to choose between God and man. If you have chosen to follow Jesus, then follow His commandment. You *must* come out from among them. Separate yourself. Follow *your* leader. Stay with the sheep!

Faith

*For by grace are ye saved through faith; and that not of yourselves:
it is the gift of God:*

—Ephesians 2:8

CHAPTER 11

Faith Fables

Faith is the true starting point of our relationship with Jesus Christ. We would not take the first step toward salvation without some measure of faith that Jesus can and will save us. However, after carefully examining the Word of God, it should be clear that it takes more than faith alone to establish our salvation.

How is it, then, that so many Christians have come to believe that Jesus Christ offers us a doctrine of salvation based on faith alone? Let's examine some of the most common faith fables and compare them to the Word of God to find the answer.

Fable: We are saved by faith alone.

One passage in particular that is commonly used to promote this fable is Romans 10:9-10. It says:

> *That if thou shalt confess with thy mouth the Lord Jesus, and shalt believe in thine heart that God hath raised him from the dead, thou shalt be saved.*

For with the heart man believeth unto righteousness; and with the mouth confession is made unto salvation.

This passage is the foundation for the Sinner's Prayer of Salvation mentioned in a previous chapter. If we look no further than this passage, we could reasonably conclude that faith alone is sufficient for our salvation. However, we cannot hang our hopes of salvation on fragmented portions of the Bible and isolated Scriptures taken out of context.

Let's read Romans 10:1-17 to see what is says before and after those verses. It says:

Brethren, my heart's desire and prayer to God for Israel is, that they might be saved.

For I bear them record that they have a zeal of God, but not according to knowledge.

For they being ignorant of God's righteousness, and going about to establish their own righteousness, have not submitted themselves unto the righteousness of God.

For Christ is the end of the law for righteousness to every one that believeth.

For Moses describeth the righteousness which is of the law, That the man which doeth those things shall live by them.

But the righteousness which is of faith speaketh on this wise, Say not in thine heart, Who shall ascend into heaven? (that is, to bring Christ down from above:)

Or, Who shall descend into the deep? (that is, to bring up Christ again from the dead.)

But what saith it? The word is nigh thee, even in thy mouth, and in thy heart: that is, the word of faith, which we preach;

That if thou shalt confess with thy mouth the Lord Jesus, and shalt believe in thine heart that God hath raised him from the dead, thou shalt be saved.

For with the heart man believeth unto righteousness; and with the mouth confession is made unto salvation.

For the scripture saith, Whosoever believeth on him shall not be ashamed.

For there is no difference between the Jew and the Greek: for the same Lord over all is rich unto all that call upon him.

For whosoever shall call upon the name of the Lord shall be saved.

How then shall they call on him in whom they have not believed? and how shall they believe in him of whom they have not heard? and how shall they hear without a preacher?

And how shall they preach, except they be sent? as it is written, How beautiful are the feet of them that preach the gospel of peace, and bring glad tidings of good things!

But they have not all obeyed the gospel. For Esaias saith, Lord, who hath believed our report?

So then faith cometh by hearing, and hearing by the word of God.

So, what is the real message in this passage? Is the message that it takes nothing more than a verbal confession of our faith in Jesus Christ to enter into the kingdom of God? No, that is not the message. Unfortunately, when we do not look at the broader context of Romans 10, it is easy for Romans 10:9-10 to be used to convince us that faith is the only requirement for our salvation. Now, let's examine the real message.

In the first four verses, we learn that Paul has a sincere desire to see Israel saved. He acknowledges their zeal for God, but he also indicates that they do not understand the righteousness of God and the fullness of our salvation through Jesus Christ. Paul continues to speak about being saved by faith. He explains that we cannot call upon Jesus unless we are properly taught by preachers who are sent from God.

As the passage progresses, we see that they had been taught the Gospel and it had been preached to them. However, the real issue is found in Romans 10:16 which says, "But they have not all obeyed the gospel."

They have not obeyed?

What is there to obey if all we need is faith? When we confess with our mouths that Jesus is Lord and believe with our hearts unto righteousness, we must also obey what Jesus instructs us to do.

Hebrews 5:9 makes that point abundantly clear. This is what it says is required of those who will receive salvation:

> *And being made perfect, he became the author of eternal salvation unto all them that obey him;*

It takes more than just believing in Jesus to receive salvation from Him. The Bible tells us in James 2:19 that even devils believe God and tremble. We, however, must have faith, believe God, and faithfully *obey* Him in order to be saved.

Only when we have obeyed Jesus can we confess that He is our Lord and that our hearts have believed unto righteousness. Without obedience, there is no righteousness. That is especially true concerning our salvation. If our hearts are truly righteous toward God, we will believe what Jesus says. We will confess our beliefs with our mouths, and our sincere belief and confession will move us to obedience.

Another Scripture that is often used to support the salvation by faith alone message is John 3:16. It is one of the most well-known Scriptures in the Bible. It says:

> *For God so loved the world, that he gave his only begotten Son, that whosoever believeth in him should not perish, but have everlasting life.*

Is that statement true? Yes. We will be saved if we believe in Jesus Christ. If we read John 3:16 as a stand alone Scripture, again, we could reasonably conclude that faith in Jesus Christ is all that is required for our salvation. However, when we examine the complete passage, we see that John 3:16 is a single verse taken from a conversation Jesus was having with Nicodemus.

If we read the preceding verses, we will find what Jesus said to Nicodemus in the same conversation in John 3:3-5:

> *Jesus answered and said unto him, Verily, verily, I say unto thee, Except a man be born again, he cannot see the kingdom of God.*
>
> *Nicodemus saith unto him, How can a man be born when he is old? can he enter the second time into his mother's womb, and be born?*
>
> *Jesus answered, Verily, verily, I say unto thee, Except a man be born of water and of the Spirit, he cannot enter into the kingdom of God.*

We must read Jesus' entire conversation with Nicodemus to put John 3:16 into its proper context. Nowhere between John 3:5 and John 3:16 did Jesus indicate that He changed His mind about the requirement for us to be born of water and of the Spirit. We must still be born of water and of the Spirit to enter into the kingdom of God. As we see a few verses later in John 3:16, faith is also required for our salvation.

Ephesians 2:8-9 is another popular passage used by those who teach faith as the only requirement for salvation. It says:

For by grace are ye saved through faith; and that not of yourselves:
it is the gift of God:

Not of works, lest any man should boast.

These two verses are often used to suggest that the grace of God is what enables us to simply believe by faith that we are saved and no work is required of us. That is, in fact, true. No work is required of us. Jesus did all the work.

Jesus was conceived by immaculate conception, born of a virgin, and lived a completely sinless life. He built an amazing ministry that produced miracle after miracle after miracle. For all the good He did, He was publicly shamed, savagely tortured, and nailed to a cross, yet His ministry was just beginning. After dying on the cross, He soundly defeated Satan, rose from the grave, and returned with the keys of hell and death. Following His resurrection, He walked around with His disciples and many others to prove that He really had returned from the grave. When He finished His assignment on earth, He handed off the work of building the Church to His apostles. Then, He was taken up to heaven in a cloud so He could take His seat at the right hand of the throne of God.

Now that is work! It is the *work* of salvation. More importantly, it is work that not one of us could possibly do. Clearly, the only one who can ever rightfully boast about having done the work of salvation is Jesus Christ.

So, while it is true that there is no work required of us to establish our salvation, it is not true that there is no obedience required of us. By grace, Jesus did the work to give us the gift of salvation, and through obedience we must follow the instructions He gave us in order to receive it. We must still repent, be baptized in the name of Jesus Christ for the remission of our sins, be filled with God's Spirit, and have faith. Then, we will receive our free gift.

One reason we are often confused by some of the faith Scriptures is that we fail to consider the intended audience of a particular message. It is important to understand that much of the New Testament was written to the saints of the Church – people who were already saved. They had already been taught the basics of repentance, water baptism, baptism of the Spirit, and faith, and they had already taken the steps necessary to secure their salvation.

For example, Ephesians 2:8-9 which we just examined was not written to people who were inquiring about what was required to establish their salvation. When we look at the greeting in Ephesians 1, we see how Paul opens his letter. Ephesians 1:1-7 says:

> *Paul, an apostle of Jesus Christ by the will of God, to the saints which are at Ephesus, and to the faithful in Christ Jesus:*
>
> *Grace be to you, and peace, from God our Father, and from the Lord Jesus Christ.*
>
> *Blessed be the God and Father of our Lord Jesus Christ, who hath blessed us with all spiritual blessings in heavenly places in Christ:*
>
> *According as he hath chosen us in him before the foundation of the world, that we should be holy and without blame before him in love:*
>
> *Having predestinated us unto the adoption of children by Jesus Christ to himself, according to the good pleasure of his will,*
>
> *To the praise of the glory of his grace, wherein he hath made us accepted in the beloved.*
>
> *In whom we have redemption through his blood, the forgiveness of sins, according to the riches of his grace;*

It is clear from Paul's opening greeting that he was addressing people who were saints in the Church. In the last verse of this passage, we see that these individuals had already been redeemed by the blood of Jesus. Since Paul was addressing people who were already saved, it was not necessary for him to explain to them the fundamentals of salvation. In that context, what he says makes sense. They were saved by grace. Their salvation had already been established as the gift of God, and they could not boast of works because Jesus did all the real work.

In Ephesians, we examined the message about salvation that was delivered to people who were already saved. Now, let's examine four stories in Acts that reflect the explanation of salvation that was delivered to people who were not yet saved.

First, let's examine what Peter said to the unsaved people in Acts 2. They realized that they had greatly offended God when they mocked the baptism of the Spirit at Pentecost, so they asked Peter what they needed to do. In Acts 2:37-40, we see how Peter addressed that audience:

> *Now when they heard this, they were pricked in their heart, and said unto Peter and to the rest of the apostles, Men and brethren, what shall we do?*
>
> *Then Peter said unto them, Repent, and be baptized every one of you in the name of Jesus Christ for the remission of sins, and ye shall receive the gift of the Holy Ghost.*
>
> *For the promise is unto you, and to your children, and to all that are afar off, even as many as the LORD our God shall call.*
>
> *And with many other words did he testify and exhort, saying, Save yourselves from this untoward generation.*

Then, we see how these individuals respond to Peter's instructions. Acts 2:41-47 continues with this account:

> *Then they that gladly received his word were baptized: and the same day there were added unto them about three thousand souls.*
>
> *And they continued stedfastly in the apostles' doctrine and fellowship, and in breaking of bread, and in prayers.*

And fear came upon every soul: and many wonders and signs were done by the apostles.

And all that believed were together, and had all things common;

And sold their possessions and goods, and parted them to all men, as every man had need.

And they, continuing daily with one accord in the temple, and breaking bread from house to house, did eat their meat with gladness and singleness of heart,

Praising God, and having favour with all the people. And the Lord added to the church daily such as should be saved.

The ones who gladly received what Peter said promptly followed his instructions. They were baptized, they continued steadfastly in the apostles' doctrine, they remained in fellowship with other believers, and new people were saved and added to the Church daily.

In Acts 8, we find the story of the Ethiopian eunuch who was found sitting in his chariot reading the Scriptures. When Philip approached him and asked if he understood what he was reading, he indicated that he did not. He humbly acknowledged that he needed someone to teach him, so Philip proceeded to instruct him as we see in Acts 8:35-39:

Then Philip opened his mouth, and began at the same scripture, and preached unto him Jesus.

And as they went on their way, they came unto a certain water: and the eunuch said, See, here is water; what doth hinder me to be baptized?

*And Philip said, If thou believest with all thine heart, thou mayest.
And he answered and said, I believe that Jesus Christ is the Son of
God.*

*And he commanded the chariot to stand still: and they went down
both into the water, both Philip and the eunuch; and he baptized
him.*

*And when they were come up out of the water, the Spirit of the Lord
caught away Philip, that the eunuch saw him no more: and he went
on his way rejoicing.*

From his conversation with Philip, the eunuch understood what he needed
to do, and as soon as he spotted water, he got baptized.

In Acts 9, we find the story of the baptism of the apostle Paul who, prior to
his conversion, was known as Saul of Tarsus. All who believe that Paul taught
faith in Jesus Christ as the only requirement for salvation will want to pay
close attention to the details of this story.

We reviewed the first few verses of Saul's encounter with Jesus on the road
to Damascus in a previous chapter. However, those verses are worth repeat-
ing as we examine the rest of the story. This is what Acts 9:1-20 says:

*And Saul, yet breathing out threatenings and slaughter against the
disciples of the Lord, went unto the high priest,*

*And desired of him letters to Damascus to the synagogues, that if he
found any of this way, whether they were men or women, he might
bring them bound unto Jerusalem.*

*And as he journeyed, he came near Damascus: and suddenly there
shined round about him a light from heaven:*

*And he fell to the earth, and heard a voice saying unto him, Saul,
Saul, why persecutest thou me?*

And he said, Who art thou, Lord? And the Lord said, I am Jesus whom thou persecutest: it is hard for thee to kick against the pricks.

And he trembling and astonished said, Lord, what wilt thou have me to do? And the Lord said unto him, Arise, and go into the city, and it shall be told thee what thou must do.

And the men which journeyed with him stood speechless, hearing a voice, but seeing no man.

And Saul arose from the earth; and when his eyes were opened, he saw no man: but they led him by the hand, and brought him into Damascus.

And he was three days without sight, and neither did eat nor drink.

And there was a certain disciple at Damascus, named Ananias; and to him said the Lord in a vision, Ananias. And he said, Behold, I am here, Lord.

And the Lord said unto him, Arise, and go into the street which is called Straight, and enquire in the house of Judas for one called Saul, of Tarsus: for, behold, he prayeth,

And hath seen in a vision a man named Ananias coming in, and putting his hand on him, that he might receive his sight.

Then Ananias answered, Lord, I have heard by many of this man, how much evil he hath done to thy saints at Jerusalem:

And here he hath authority from the chief priests to bind all that call on thy name.

But the Lord said unto him, Go thy way: for he is a chosen vessel unto me, to bear my name before the Gentiles, and kings, and the children of Israel:

For I will shew him how great things he must suffer for my name's sake.

And Ananias went his way, and entered into the house; and putting his hands on him said, Brother Saul, the Lord, even Jesus, that appeared unto thee in the way as thou camest, hath sent me, that thou mightest receive thy sight, and be filled with the Holy Ghost.

And immediately there fell from his eyes as it had been scales: and he received sight forthwith, and arose, and was baptized.

And when he had received meat, he was strengthened. Then was Saul certain days with the disciples which were at Damascus.

And straightway he preached Christ in the synagogues, that he is the Son of God.

Saul certainly acknowledged his faith in Jesus Christ as Lord while on the road to Damascus. Nonetheless, Jesus made it clear that there was something more that he needed to do. He sent Saul to the city to wait for Ananias whom He handpicked to deliver His instructions. The message Ananias delivered to Saul upon first meeting him is the same message Jesus delivered to Nicodemus in John 3:3-5.

Jesus told Nicodemus that in order to be born again and enter the kingdom of God we must be born of water and born of the Spirit. Ananias laid hands on Saul and advised him that he would receive his sight again and be filled with the Holy Ghost. As soon as Saul regained his sight, it only took him a split second to run to the water and get baptized.

We have examined what Saul was told by Jesus while on the road to Damascus and what he was later told by Ananias. We have examined what he did in response to the instruction he was given. Now, let's examine what he later wrote after becoming the apostle Paul concerning his understanding of the requirements for salvation. We find it in Titus 3:3-7:

> *For we ourselves also were sometimes foolish, disobedient, deceived, serving divers lusts and pleasures, living in malice and envy, hateful, and hating one another.*
>
> *But after that the kindness and love of God our Saviour toward man appeared,*
>
> *Not by works of righteousness which we have done, but according to his mercy he saved us, by the washing of regeneration, and renewing of the Holy Ghost;*
>
> *Which he shed on us abundantly through Jesus Christ our Saviour;*
>
> *That being justified by his grace, we should be made heirs according to the hope of eternal life.*

In this passage we see exactly what Paul believed about how we are saved. We are not saved by our own works of righteousness. According to God's mercy, He saved us by the washing of regeneration and the renewing of the Holy Ghost. The washing of regeneration is water baptism. The renewing of the Holy Ghost is the baptism of the Spirit. That is what Jesus said, that is what Paul was told by Ananias, and that is what Paul later wrote in Titus.

Now let's examine the final story which is found in Acts 16:25-34. It is the story of the Philippian jail keeper. The Bible says:

> *And at midnight Paul and Silas prayed, and sang praises unto God: and the prisoners heard them.*

And suddenly there was a great earthquake, so that the foundations of the prison were shaken: and immediately all the doors were opened, and every one's bands were loosed.

And the keeper of the prison awaking out of his sleep, and seeing the prison doors open, he drew out his sword, and would have killed himself, supposing that the prisoners had been fled.

But Paul cried with a loud voice, saying, Do thyself no harm: for we are all here.

Then he called for a light, and sprang in, and came trembling, and fell down before Paul and Silas,

And brought them out, and said, Sirs, what must I do to be saved?

And they said, Believe on the Lord Jesus Christ, and thou shalt be saved, and thy house.

And they spake unto him the word of the Lord, and to all that were in his house.

And he took them the same hour of the night, and washed their stripes; and was baptized, he and all his, straightway.

And when he had brought them into his house, he set meat before them, and rejoiced, believing in God with all his house.

When the jail keeper saw the power of God shake the earth and throw open the prison doors to release Paul and Silas, he only had one question: What must I do to be saved?

Paul certainly knew the answer after recently asking essentially the same question of Jesus during their encounter on the road to Damascus. Paul and Silas told him exactly what he needed to do to be saved.

First, they explained that he needed to put his faith in Jesus Christ. Next, they proceeded to explain the rest of what he and his household must do. When they finished delivering the message, the jailer and his entire household got baptized. They could have waited until daybreak, but they didn't. They all got baptized that same hour in the middle of the night. They ran to the water just as Saul did as soon as he regained his sight.

We have examined the record. In four stories in Acts, we see a clear and consistent pattern among people who desperately wanted to be saved. Those who believed on Pentecost went from ridiculing and mocking the baptism of the Spirit to being baptized that same day. After learning of salvation, the Ethiopian eunuch got baptized as soon as he saw water. Paul got baptized as soon as the scales fell from his eyes. The jailer keeper went from being on the verge of committing suicide to getting baptized along with his entire household.

So, are we saved by faith and grace alone? Absolutely not. Do the Scriptures that tell us we are saved by faith and grace contradict what is communicated in Acts? Absolutely not.

What is written in Ephesians about being saved by faith is absolutely correct – if it is directed to people who are already saved. All they need for salvation is to continue to walk in faith – if they have already repented, been baptized in the name of Jesus Christ, and received the baptism of the Spirit.

The message that is consistently communicated in the stories we read in Acts is also absolutely correct - if it is directed to an unsaved person who wants to understand what they must do to be saved. That person needs to hear God's entire plan of salvation, not just the portion concerning faith.

Unfortunately, many people quote Scriptures from books written by Paul to dispute what Jesus said. We, however, must understand this simple truth - Paul is not the author of salvation. He was only a messenger of the Gospel that was entrusted to him by Jesus Christ. Everything he wrote was written under the inspiration of the Spirit of Christ and the Spirit of Jesus Christ never contradicts the Person of Jesus Christ. When we attempt to use Scriptures to prove that we are saved by faith alone, we have taken a doctrinal position on salvation that directly contradicts what Jesus taught.

Fable: Faith is the easy part of salvation.

There are only four things we need for our salvation – repentance, water baptism in the name of Jesus Christ, the baptism of the Spirit, and faith. Once we defeat the devil on the first three, he has nothing left to attack but our faith. He knows that faith is as essential to our ability to enter into eternal life as the first three requirements, so he constantly attacks us. That is why, for many people, holding onto faith is the hardest part of salvation. We must hold onto our faith by fighting for it as we see in 1 Timothy 6:12 which says:

> *Fight the good fight of faith, lay hold on eternal life, whereunto thou art also called, and hast professed a good profession before many witnesses.*

The challenges of life are inevitable, so we must fight the good fight of faith daily. If our faith is weak, we can become easily overwhelmed, uncertain, and disillusioned. We may wonder if God can or will help us with our problems. We may forget that our salvation assures us that God will always work on our behalf as long as we remain in right standing with Him. We may also lose faith when we experience guilt and condemnation after offending God with sin. When we do, we often feel unworthy of His grace and His mercy and uncertain of whether He will continue to forgive us.

When we become fearful, unbelieving, and uncertain of God's willingness or ability to help us, it is not because God has forsaken us. It is because we have lost faith in our salvation through Jesus Christ and we have, in fact, unknowingly forsaken God.

We have forgotten His goodness, His kindness, His mercy, His grace, and His faithfulness. We have forgotten His promises and lost confidence in His power. We have lost faith in the protection Jesus Christ gave us when He covered us with His blood. We have forgotten that throughout the Bible, God continually reminds us not to be afraid and He encourages us to trust Him as our Father. He comforts us and promises to never leave us nor forsake us.

If we will simply meditate on His faithfulness, His promises, and His love for us, we will learn to trust Him. More importantly, we will develop a level of faith that shows God that we understand who He is to us. This is what God says about His great love for us in 1 John 3:1:

> *Behold, what manner of love the Father hath bestowed upon us, that we should be called the sons of God: therefore the world knoweth us not, because it knew him not.*

Satan continually attacks our faith so we will forget God's love for us. As soon as we do, he draws us into fear and unbelief because he knows they are an insult to the power of the blood of Jesus. He desperately wants us to place our faith in him instead of Christ. The devil wants us to believe that his ability to harm us is greater than Jesus' desire and ability to save us. That is an absolute lie, and soon as we allow the devil to trick us into believing his lie, we have a problem with God. The problem is described in Hebrews 11:6 which says:

> *But without faith it is impossible to please him [God]: for he that cometh to God must believe that he is, and that he is a rewarder of them that diligently seek him.*

No matter what else we do, if we lose faith in the God of our salvation, it is impossible for us to please Him. In fact, God becomes so offended that He strips away His precious promises from faithless, unbelieving people. Hebrews 3:12 tells us that an unbelieving heart is evil in God's eyes. He reminds us in Hebrews 3 and 4 that He left the children of Israel to perish in the wilderness because of their evil heart of unbelief toward Him. He will do the same to us if we approach Him with fear and unbelief.

Hebrews 11, on the other hand, gives us an amazing account of the great and mighty miracles God performed for people of great faith. He will do the same for us, too, if we will have faith in Him. God will bless us in miraculous ways and give us the gift of eternal life simply for having faith in Him. That is why, just as 1 Timothy 6:12 encourages us to fight the good fight of faith and lay hold of eternal life, Ephesians 6:16 also reminds us of the importance of our faith. It says:

> *Above all, taking the shield of faith, wherewith ye shall be able to quench all the fiery darts of the wicked.*

We must stay hidden in Jesus Christ, our mighty fortress and shield of faith, trusting that He has power over all things including Satan. Not only does Jesus have all power and authority over him, so do we. Read Luke 10 and you will see. Jesus sent out seventy disciples to minister in pairs in various cities. Luke 10:17-20 gives this report of what occurred when they returned. It says:

> *And the seventy returned again with joy, saying, Lord, even the devils are subject unto us through thy name.*
>
> *And he said unto them, I beheld Satan as lightning fall from heaven.*
>
> *Behold, I give unto you power to tread on serpents and scorpions, and over all the power of the enemy: and nothing shall by any means hurt you.*
>
> *Notwithstanding in this rejoice not, that the spirits are subject unto you; but rather rejoice, because your names are written in heaven.*

The most important thing for us to remember about the devil is that he is not worthy to receive anything Jesus has for us including one single drop of our faith. When we are covered by the blood that has already defeated him, we have nothing to fear. He, on the other hand, has much to fear. His eternal fate is signed and sealed. This is what Revelation 20:10 says about his eternal destiny:

> *And the devil that deceived them was cast into the lake of fire and brimstone, where the beast and the false prophet are, and shall be tormented day and night for ever and ever.*

Jesus came to take us to heaven. That is where we are going and we are going to hold onto our faith in Him until we get there. Until then, we are to take dominion over the devil and everything he attempts to bring against us. He *must* bow down to the name of Jesus Christ and he *will* when we exercise the power God has given us.

Keep the faith!

Fable: Sometimes it is impossible to develop enough faith to overcome our greatest fears.

Fear and unbelief are sins. There is no sin that God has not given us the power to overcome. We must be fiercely determined to overcome fear and unbelief because this is what Revelation 21:7-8 says will happen if we fail to do so:

> *He that overcometh shall inherit all things; and I will be his God, and he shall be my son.*

> *But the fearful, and unbelieving, and the abominable, and murderers, and whoremongers, and sorcerers, and idolaters, and all liars, shall have their part in the lake which burneth with fire and brimstone: which is the second death.*

The first step toward overcoming fear which often leads to unbelief is to understand that fear is a state of mind created by a spirit. This is what God tells us about that spirit in 2 Timothy 1:7:

> *For God hath not given us the spirit of fear; but of power, and of love, and of a sound mind.*

Once we understand that fear is created by a spirit, we must also understand that faith cannot coexist with that spirit. Faith must cast out the spirit of fear, or the spirit of fear will cast out our faith. So how do we keep the power, love, and soundness of mind that God gives us when we are attacked by the spirit of fear?

As soon as we begin to sense that we are becoming anxious and fearful about anything, we must recognize that we are being attacked by the spirit of fear. Then, we must immediately respond by fighting against it. We fight by using God's Spirit to help us build the type of faith that casts out fear. Jude 1:20-21 tells us how to do that. It says:

> *But ye, beloved, building up yourselves on your most holy faith, praying in the Holy Ghost,*
>
> *Keep yourselves in the love of God, looking for the mercy of our Lord Jesus Christ unto eternal life.*

When we pray in the Holy Ghost by speaking in tongues, the Spirit of Christ builds up our most holy faith. As our faith increases, we begin to actively experience the presence of God's power and His love again. We feel ourselves becoming more hopeful and confident, trusting that God has a plan and that everything will work in our favor. It becomes easier to abide in the peace of God and trust in His Word rather than believing the lies being whispered to us by the spirit of fear.

As we continue to pray in the Holy Ghost, the spirit of fear is cast out by our faith, and our minds begin to recover from the spiritual attack. Soon we find that we are able to operate with the soundness of mind that we cannot access when we are being tormented by fear. Eventually, we are able to again abide in the peaceful mental state described in Isaiah 26:3. It says:

> *Thou wilt keep him in perfect peace, whose mind is stayed on thee: because he trusteth in thee.*

The frequency and duration of our prayers will be determined by the frequency and severity of the spiritual attacks waged against us by the spirit of fear. We must simply learn to fight by praying as often and as long as necessary to overcome fear and abide in the love and peace of God. Through disciplined consistency in our response to the spirit of fear, God will teach us to master the warfare of building our most holy faith.

Expect the trials of life to come. When they do, expect your faith to be tested and challenged by the spirit of fear. Just remember that no matter what circumstances we face, God has given us the power of the Holy Ghost so we can enjoy fearless living.

When we build up our most holy faith by praying in the Holy Ghost, we will experience God's perfect love. That love will cast out all fear because that is what God promised us in 1 John 4:18. It says:

> *There is no fear in love; but perfect love casteth out fear: because fear hath torment. He that feareth is not made perfect in love.*

Each time our faith is tested, we must remind ourselves that it is an open book test. There is only one question on the test and God has already given us the only answer that He will accept.

In Jeremiah 32:27, God asks the question:

> *Behold, I am the Lord, the God of all flesh: is there any thing too hard for me?*

And, in Luke 1:37, He gives us the answer:

> *For with God nothing shall be impossible.*

CHAPTER 12

The Ultimate Faith Fable

I hope and pray that we have examined enough fables and biblical truths to convince you of one thing. If you hear, believe, and obey fables, you will miss salvation. Before we examine the final fable, however, I believe it is important that we end our study of fables where we began – with a reminder of this truth.

We are in a war. We are fighting for two things. Lives. Souls.

Jesus came to give us the abundant life on earth and to preserve our souls through eternal life in heaven. Satan came to steal, kill, and destroy our lives and our souls. Our ability to secure what Jesus died to give us is facilitated through the practical application of biblical truth. If we miss the truth, we risk missing everything Jesus Christ died for. That is why we cannot miss the truth about this fable.

Fable: I have faith that once I'm saved, I cannot lose my salvation.

One of the most dangerous fables of all is that once we are saved, we are always saved. Many churches teach that we can never lose our salvation.

Consequently, that is what many people believe. Let's closely examine this fable.

The root can be traced back to John 10:27-29. In that passage of Scripture, this is what Jesus said:

My sheep hear my voice, and I know them, and they follow me:

And I give unto them eternal life; and they shall never perish, neither shall any man pluck them out of my hand.

My Father, which gave them me, is greater than all; and no man is able to pluck them out of my Father's hand.

People often read this passage of Scripture and focus on the promise of never losing eternal life. They are comforted in knowing that no man can pluck them out of Jesus' hand. Those are comforting thoughts for anyone.

However, as we have seen with many other Scriptures, it is unwise to draw a conclusion from a few isolated verses about something as important as the eternal fate of our souls. When we examine these three verses against other Scriptures, it becomes clear that there are conditions associated with maintaining our salvation.

Read the passage again. In the first verse you will find two significant points that people often miss. The first verse tells us two things about sheep. Sheep know the voice of their Shepherd *and* they follow Him. Sheep who know the voice of their Shepherd and willingly choose to follow Him can expect to arrive safely inside the gates of heaven. The Good Shepherd will lead them there.

However, Romans 8:14 tells us this:

For as many as are led by the Spirit of God, they are the sons of God.

As long as we choose to follow God and be led by His Spirit, we are His sons and daughters. However, God gives each of us free will. Just as we choose to leave the kingdom of darkness and enter into the kingdom of God, we can choose to change our minds about our salvation.

We can choose to forsake God, follow Satan back into a life of sin, and return to darkness and bondage. Those who make that choice are no longer being led by God's Spirit, they are no longer sons and daughters of God, and they are no longer sheep. They become goats again, and goats do not inherit eternal life. When, exactly, do sheep become goats again? Whenever God grows sufficiently weary of their failure to repent. When He does, He cuts them off from their inheritance and returns them to their chosen kingdom and their chosen ruler who is the devil.

So, the passage is true. No man can pluck us from Jesus' hand. However, through our own free will, we can certainly choose to leave the safety and security of His hand. Those who make that choice forfeit their salvation.

Now, let's examine three passages of Scripture that sternly warn us about the possibility of losing our salvation and two stories that clearly illustrate the point.

The first Scripture is in Philippians. However, before we examine it, it is important to note that Philippians is a letter written to a particular audience – the Church. We can determine that from the manner in which the letter begins.

Philippians 1:1 says:

> *Paul and Timotheus, the servants of Jesus Christ, to all the saints in Christ Jesus which are at Philippi, with the bishops and deacons:*

Saints, bishops, and deacons are people who are saved and in the Church. They are sheep. Now consider this stern warning given to that audience later in Philippians 2:12:

> *Wherefore, my beloved, as ye have always obeyed, not as in my presence only, but now much more in my absence, work out your own salvation with fear and trembling.*

Work out your own salvation? With fear and trembling?

Perhaps you're wondering, "Work? What work? I thought saved people have an unconditional guarantee of smooth sailing all the way to heaven!"

Well, apparently not. If we had an unconditional guarantee of smooth sailing all the way to heaven, there would be no need for fear and trembling among the saints, bishops, and deacons.

The truth is that there are no unconditional guarantees of smooth sailing all the way to heaven on God's boat. Jesus did the work necessary to offer us the gift of salvation. Our work begins as soon as we accept His gift. That is precisely why the Bible instructs us to work out our salvation with fear and trembling. The only sheep who are guaranteed safe sailing all the way to heaven are those who hear, believe, and obey God's Word for the duration of their journey. We all must diligently work to consistently make godly choices in every area of our lives. We must quickly repent when we fail to do so and be determined to make better choices going forward. Ongoing obedience is the reasonable service God requires for us to maintain our salvation.

Philippians 2:12 alone is enough to convince me that the security of our salvation is contingent upon our ongoing obedience. However, it is important that we examine the Bible to find additional support for that position. We find it in Hebrews 6:4-6 which says:

> *For it is impossible for those who were once enlightened, and have tasted of the heavenly gift, and were made partakers of the Holy Ghost,*

> *And have tasted the good word of God, and the powers of the world to come,*

> *If they shall fall away, to renew them again unto repentance; seeing they crucify to themselves the Son of God afresh, and put him to an open shame.*

The first verse in this passage makes it clear that the Bible again is referring to people who are saved. We know that because they are referred to as people who "were made partakers of the Holy Ghost." The passage clearly states that if those individuals fall away, it is impossible to renew them again unto repentance.

We established earlier in our study on repentance that God can and will eventually lose patience with us. We saw it in Jeremiah 15:6 which says:

> *Thou hast forsaken me, saith the Lord, thou art gone backward: therefore will I stretch out my hand against thee, and destroy thee; I am weary with repenting.*

Now, in Hebrews 6:4-6, we see the same message applies to people who are saved and filled with the Holy Ghost. We know that without repentance, God does not cleanse us of our sins. Without having our sins cleansed, we cannot get into heaven.

That is why it is so important for us to keep our hearts perfect toward God. As His sheep, we must diligently study His Word. In doing so, we will become so sensitive to His Spirit that we feel the slightest tug and hear the most gentle whisper as He draws us toward repentance.

When we become desensitized to sin and harden our hearts toward God, we miss His tugs and His whispers. When we miss enough of those tugs and whispers, we risk being put off the boat and no longer counted among the sheep.

We see that in Romans 11:20-23 in Paul's letter to the sheep in Rome:

> *Well; because of unbelief they were broken off, and thou standest by faith. Be not highminded, but fear:*
>
> *For if God spared not the natural branches, take heed lest he also spare not thee.*
>
> *Behold therefore the goodness and severity of God: on them which fell, severity; but toward thee, goodness, if thou continue in his goodness: otherwise thou also shalt be cut off.*

And they also, if they abide not still in unbelief, shall be grafted in: for God is able to graft them in again.

In this passage, Paul issues a serious warning to Gentile believers about God's goodness and severity. He explains that Jews who have not accepted Jesus Christ can be grafted into the Body of Christ if they accept Him as Lord and Savior. Conversely, Gentiles who have been grafted in through their acceptance of Jesus Christ will be cut off if they do not continue in God's goodness.

Yes, He is a God of mercy, kindness, and grace. He is also a God of severity for those who choose to ignore the voice of the Shepherd. It takes hard work, diligent study, and prompt repentance to remain in right standing with God. We must faithfully obey Him throughout our journey until we make it safely through the gates.

God clearly makes that point through the stories of Hymenaeus, Ananias, and Sapphira. These three individuals were once saved and living their lives as sheep. The great question that remains to be answered is whether they died saved. I encourage you to examine their stories and decide for yourself.

Hymenaeus

In Paul's first letter to Timothy, he writes about Hymenaeus. This is what he says in 1 Timothy 1:18-20:

> *This charge I commit unto thee, son Timothy, according to the prophecies which went before on thee, that thou by them mightest war a good warfare;*

> *Holding faith, and a good conscience; which some having put away concerning faith have made shipwreck:*

> *Of whom is Hymenaeus and Alexander; whom I have delivered unto Satan, that they may learn not to blaspheme.*

Later, in 2 Timothy 2:15-26 , we see that Paul makes a second reference to Hymeneaus.

Study to shew thyself approved unto God, a workman that needeth not to be ashamed, rightly dividing the word of truth.

But shun profane and vain babblings: for they will increase unto more ungodliness.

And their word will eat as doth a canker: of whom is Hymenaeus and Philetus;

Who concerning the truth have erred, saying that the resurrection is past already; and overthrow the faith of some.

Nevertheless the foundation of God standeth sure, having this seal, The Lord knoweth them that are his. And, let every one that nameth the name of Christ depart from iniquity.

But in a great house there are not only vessels of gold and of silver, but also of wood and of earth; and some to honour, and some to dishonor.

If a man therefore purge himself from these, he shall be a vessel unto honour, sanctified, and meet for the master's use, and prepared unto every good work.

Flee also youthful lusts: but follow righteousness, faith, charity, peace, with them that call on the Lord out of a pure heart.

But foolish and unlearned questions avoid, knowing that they do gender strifes.

And the servant of the Lord must not strive; but be gentle unto all men, apt to teach, patient,

In meekness instructing those that oppose themselves; if God peradventure will give them repentance to the acknowledging of the truth;

And that they may recover themselves out of the snare of the devil, who are taken captive by him at his will.

In the first passage, we see that, according to Paul, Hymenaeus was once in the faith. However, because of his sin, Paul handed him over to Satan. In the last two verses of this second passage, note what the Bible tells us.

There is no guarantee that those who were once saved will be granted repentance so they can recover themselves from the snares of the devil. Their ability to recover is conditional upon God's willingness to grant them repentance.

Was Hymenaeus saved? Absolutely. Was he later handed over to Satan? Absolutely. Did God grant him repentance so he could recover himself from the snare of the devil? Maybe. Maybe not. If God did not grant him repentance, did he make it to heaven?

Ananias and Sapphira

Next, consider Ananias and Sapphira, a husband and wife whose story we should know. They belonged to a community of believers that is described in Acts 4:32-37. This is what it says:

And the multitude of them that believed were of one heart and of one soul: neither said any of them that ought of the things which he possessed was his own; but they had all things common.

And with great power gave the apostles witness of the resurrection of the Lord Jesus: and great grace was upon them all.

Neither was there any among them that lacked: for as many as were possessors of lands or houses sold them, and brought the prices of the things that were sold,

And laid them down at the apostles' feet: and distribution was made unto every man according as he had need.

And Joses, who by the apostles was surnamed Barnabas, (which is, being interpreted, The son of consolation,) a Levite, and of the country of Cyprus,

Having land, sold it, and brought the money, and laid it at the apostles' feet.

This was a community of people who had one heart, one soul, and the Spirit of Christ was their common bond. As we continue reading in Acts 5:1-11, we find the details of what occurred with this couple and their community:

But a certain man named Ananias, with Sapphira his wife, sold a possession,

And kept back part of the price, his wife also being privy to it, and brought a certain part, and laid it at the apostles' feet.

But Peter said, Ananias, why hath Satan filled thine heart to lie to the Holy Ghost, and to keep back part of the price of the land?

Whiles it remained, was it not thine own? and after it was sold, was it not in thine own power? why hast thou conceived this thing in thine heart? thou hast not lied unto men, but unto God.

And Ananias hearing these words fell down, and gave up the ghost: and great fear came on all them that heard these things.

And the young men arose, wound him up, and carried him out, and buried him.

And it was about the space of three hours after, when his wife, not knowing what was done, came in.

And Peter answered unto her, Tell me whether ye sold the land for so much? And she said, Yea, for so much.

Then Peter said unto her, How is it that ye have agreed together to tempt the Spirit of the Lord? behold, the feet of them which have buried thy husband are at the door, and shall carry thee out.

Then fell she down straightway at his feet, and yielded up the ghost: and the young men came in, and found her dead, and, carrying her forth, buried her by her husband.

And great fear came upon all the church, and upon as many as heard these things.

Clearly, Ananias and Sapphira were saved, yet they allowed Satan to fill their hearts and entice them into lying to the Holy Ghost. They offended God so greatly that He killed them on the spot in the presence of their neighbors. Ananias and Sapphira died because they failed to work out their salvation with fear and trembling.

What we know with certainty about Ananias and Sapphira is why they died. What we do not know with certainty is whether God granted them repentance before they died. If He did, He certainly left no record of it. That is why the last verse of their story is well worth remembering.

Great fear came upon all the church then just as it should come upon all of us in the Church today. God certainly wants us to be comforted in knowing that He is still a God of goodness just as He always has been. However, He also expects us to remember that He is still a God of great severity when He is deeply offended.

I do not take the deaths of Ananias and Sapphira lightly. They were saved people who fell prey to the tricks and traps of the devil and they paid dearly for their life choices. If they had young children, their precious children became orphans, losing both parents within a matter of three hours. Even if they had no children, they certainly must have had friends and loved ones who were deeply grieved by their loss. I believe God left us their story to help us understand that salvation is not a sure pass into heaven for everyone who gets saved. It is only a sure pass into heaven for everyone who gets saved, lives saved, and dies saved.

PART 3

Wise Choices

And if it seem evil unto you to serve the LORD, choose you this day whom ye will serve; whether the gods which your fathers served that were on the other side of the flood, or the gods of the Amorites, in whose land ye dwell: but as for me and my house, we will serve the LORD.

—Joshua 24:15

CHAPTER 13

Choose Truth

Perhaps you have encountered some new truths in your journey through this book and the Word of God. Some may be easy to accept, and others may be thoroughly disruptive to your belief system. That was certainly the case for me. Some of the truths I encountered were a bit unsettling, some were wholly disruptive, and others seemed completely unbelievable.

I wrestled with some of those truths for a long time, knowing that in order for me to be completely at peace with God, something had to change. Eventually, I had to accept that no matter how long I wrestled, the truth was not going to change. That left me with three choices. I could continue to wrestle with the unchanging truth, I could walk away from it, or I could accept it. I made my choice based on John 8:31-32. It says:

> *Then said Jesus to those Jews which believed on him, If ye continue in my word, then are ye my disciples indeed;*
>
> *And ye shall know the truth, and the truth shall make you free.*

I chose to be a disciple of Jesus Christ and I chose to be free. In the process of learning to embrace disruptive truths, I did a great deal of self-examination and soul searching. I wondered how it was possible that I could have missed simple, foundational teachings for so long. After all, I had read the Word of God. I had diligently studied it for many years. I had taught many people. Finally, one day, God freed me from my search for answers with three simple words: "Get over it."

God has an appointed time for everything including an appointed time for each of us to receive knowledge and understanding of truth. God will open our eyes to the truth when He is ready for us to see it. If we do not harden our hearts toward Him, we will see exactly what He wants us to see exactly when He wants us to see it.

The apostle Paul's story provides a classic example that perfectly illustrates that point. As Saul, he was an extremely well educated, highly regarded religious leader. He certainly had heard the truth from the apostles. In fact, it was the truth they taught that made him so determined to zealously persecute them and other followers of Christ. So, if he heard the truth, why did he not see it? He was unquestionably a brilliant scholar. In fact, this is how he later describes himself in Philippians 3:3-9:

> *For we are the circumcision, which worship God in the spirit, and rejoice in Christ Jesus, and have no confidence in the flesh.*
>
> *Though I might also have confidence in the flesh. If any other man thinketh that he hath whereof he might trust in the flesh, I more:*
>
> *Circumcised the eighth day, of the stock of Israel, of the tribe of Benjamin, an Hebrew of the Hebrews; as touching the law, a Pharisee;*
>
> *Concerning zeal, persecuting the church; touching the righteousness which is in the law, blameless.*
>
> *But what things were gain to me, those I counted loss for Christ.*

Yea doubtless, and I count all things but loss for the excellency of the knowledge of Christ Jesus my Lord: for whom I have suffered the loss of all things, and do count them but dung, that I may win Christ,

And be found in him, not having mine own righteousness, which is of the law, but that which is through the faith of Christ, the righteousness which is of God by faith:

Clearly, Paul's pedigree was impeccable. So why did he miss the truth? He missed it because God's appointed time had not yet arrived for his eyes to be opened. His time did not arrive until he encountered Jesus on the road to Damascus. Then he got it!

Paul received a whole new revelation about the truth in that encounter with Jesus Christ. The truth he gladly received eventually led him to make a humbling confession. He acknowledged that all those things that once established him as a highly regarded religious leader were worth no more than dung to him in comparison to the salvation he gained after learning the truth.

Unlike the apostle Paul, however, the apostles Peter and John were not at all well educated. Acts 4:13 describes how they were perceived by religious leaders like Paul. It says:

Now when they saw the boldness of Peter and John, and perceived that they were unlearned and ignorant men, they marvelled; and they took knowledge of them, that they had been with Jesus.

Peter and John lacked Paul's pedigree and their presentation was unimpressive. Yet, despite being perceived as unlearned and ignorant, they got it. So how did Peter and John get it when Paul missed it?

It's simple. Despite the perception that Peter and John were unlearned and ignorant men, they were, in fact, quite well educated. They received an exceptional education from Jesus Christ. Jesus revealed the truth to them at His appointed time and they chose to accept what He revealed. Then, He personally tutored and mentored them until He was satisfied that they were fully prepared to become leaders in His ministry.

Saul, on the other hand, had an exceptional formal education, but he had not yet received a revelation of the truth from Jesus. When the appointed time arrived, Jesus revealed the truth to him, too. Saul had to make a choice and he chose wisely. He chose to get over it. He accepted the truth, changed his longstanding doctrinal beliefs, and radically changed his ministry.

Here's the point. God's plan of salvation really is simple, but Jesus must open our eyes to the truth in order for us to see it. If Peter and John got it, anyone can get it. We don't need to go to seminary or stand in a pulpit for years to comprehend it. Conversely, regardless of our education or experience, if Saul missed the truth, anyone can miss it unless Jesus reveals it.

All we must do is pray for God to lead us into truth. When He does, we must hear, believe, and obey it, and we must fight the good fight of faith to hold onto it.

CHAPTER 14

Choose Holiness

Jesus Christ died on the cross and rose again to offer us the amazing gift of salvation. Once we choose to receive it, we must also choose to live a lifestyle that will enable us to make it all the way to heaven. That lifestyle is called holiness. We choose holiness because, as Hebrews 12:14 tells us, without holiness, no man shall see the Lord.

Unfortunately, holiness has become greatly mischaracterized. It is often portrayed as a sterile existence achieved through legalistic adherence to oppressive religious traditions. Many also portray it as a life of rigor that requires avoidance of everything joyful that exists outside the church walls. That is not the life Jesus came to give us.

Jesus came to give us an abundant life. We live that life by wholeheartedly embracing His doctrine, practices, and teachings while enjoying great liberty, freedom, and blessings. All of that abundance remains ours as long as we abide in Christ.

The Acts 2 Church gives us a glimpse of a church community comprised of people who were committed to living a joyful lifestyle of holiness. This is how that community is described in Acts 2:37-47:

Now when they heard this, they were pricked in their heart, and said unto Peter and to the rest of the apostles, Men and brethren, what shall we do?

Then Peter said unto them, Repent, and be baptized every one of you in the name of Jesus Christ for the remission of sins, and ye shall receive the gift of the Holy Ghost.

For the promise is unto you, and to your children, and to all that are afar off, even as many as the Lord our God shall call.

And with many other words did he testify and exhort, saying, Save yourselves from this untoward generation.

Then they that gladly received his word were baptized: and the same day there were added unto them about three thousand souls.

And they continued stedfastly in the apostles' doctrine and fellowship, and in breaking of bread, and in prayers.

And fear came upon every soul: and many wonders and signs were done by the apostles.

And all that believed were together, and had all things common;

And sold their possessions and goods, and parted them to all men, as every man had need.

And they, continuing daily with one accord in the temple, and breaking bread from house to house, did eat their meat with gladness and singleness of heart,

Praising God, and having favour with all the people. And the Lord added to the church daily such as should be saved.

What an amazing life! Wouldn't you love to be part of a community like that? Well, in this passage, the Bible tells us exactly how to create that kind of life.

First and foremost, if we are unsaved, we must seek the truth to learn what is necessary for us to be reconciled to God. When we hear His simple plan of salvation, we must choose to save ourselves by believing and obeying His Word. Then, we must connect with like-minded believers.

As we see in the Acts 2 Church, we need active engagement in a strong church community. In our search for the right church, however, we must remember that a house is only as strong as the foundation upon which it is built. The same is true of a church. The foundation of every church is its doctrine. That is why, before we join a church, we must carefully inspect the foundation. We must ensure it is a church that preaches and teaches no doctrine other than the apostles' doctrine. The apostles' doctrine is the true Gospel of Jesus Christ.

After we become planted in a church that we are confident is built on a foundation of sound doctrine, it is important that we make every effort to become meaningfully connected to others in our church community. Our commitment to building deep, meaningful relationships with other born again believers who are faithfully walking with God is an important part of building our relationship with Christ.

We must remain in continual fellowship with other born again believers, coming together to pray, worship, praise God, and hear the uncompromised teaching and preaching of His Word. We must encourage one another in the Lord and commit to the practical application of biblical truth in our daily lives. We must be diligent about keeping unity in the Body of Christ, remaining on one accord with our brothers and sisters in Christ. We must learn to give unselfishly of ourselves and continually walk in love, caring for one another with gladness and singleness of heart.

It may take work to find the right church. It certainly takes work to consistently make the daily choices that enable us to live a joyful life of holiness. We must remember, though, that salvation is the most important work of our lives. The good news is that, if we do the work, the rewards are great.

When we work out our own salvation with fear and trembling, we save ourselves. We position our children and our loved ones who become part of our church community to save themselves. We live abundantly and victoriously as we enjoy a daily celebration of our brand new life in Jesus Christ. Most importantly, when our celebration of life on earth is over, we and our saved loved ones will be fully prepared for the real celebration in the place Jesus has already prepared for us. This is what He says about it in John 14:1-6:

> *Let not your heart be troubled: ye believe in God, believe also in me.*
>
> *In my Father's house are many mansions: if it were not so, I would have told you. I go to prepare a place for you.*
>
> *And if I go and prepare a place for you, I will come again, and receive you unto myself; that where I am, there ye may be also.*
>
> *And whither I go ye know, and the way ye know.*
>
> *Thomas saith unto him, Lord, we know not whither thou goest; and how can we know the way?*
>
> *Jesus saith unto him, I am the way, the truth, and the life: no man cometh unto the Father, but by me.*

Just as Jesus said, you know the way. You know the way to the abundant life on earth that you will enjoy and celebrate as part of a thriving Acts 2 church community. Most importantly, you know the way to the mansion Jesus has already prepared for your eternal life in heaven!

CHAPTER 15

Choose Salvation

Repentance

+

Water Baptism in the Name of Jesus Christ

+

Baptism of the Spirit

+

Faith

=

Salvation

This simple equation summarizes God's entire plan of salvation and brings us to our final destination. This is the place where biblical truth leads us into personal truth concerning that one burning question.

Are you *really* saved?

If you are *really* saved according to the Word of God, shout, "Hallelujah!" Then, thank God for your salvation! Each day, treat it as if it is the most precious gift you will ever receive. Now, relax and rejoice in knowing with certainty that you're on God's boat! All you have to do to stay on the boat is commit to living the Acts 2 lifestyle of holiness and enjoy the rest of your journey. God has an amazing life in store for you, and when your boat ride is over, you can retire in your mansion!

If, on the other hand, you are not saved according to the Word of God, there's great news for you, too. God gave Noah instructions to help him build the boat that saved him and his entire family. He's given you instructions to help you get on a boat that will save you, too. Now that you've heard the truth, all you need to do is believe it and obey it.

What are you waiting for? The Acts 2 Party Boat is ready to set sail and God has a cabin reserved just for you. Hurry up!

Repent.

Run to the water to be baptized in the name of Jesus Christ for the remission of your sins.

Ask God for the Holy Ghost and trust that He will give it to you at His appointed time.

Now hold onto your faith, hold onto your hat, and enjoy the ride!

PART 4

One Lost Sheep

And he spake this parable unto them, saying,

What man of you, having an hundred sheep, if he lose one of them,
doth not leave the ninety and nine in the wilderness, and go after that
which is lost, until he find it?

And when he hath found it, he layeth it on his shoulders, rejoicing.

And when he cometh home, he calleth together his friends and neighbours,
saying unto them, Rejoice with me; for I have found my sheep which was lost.

I say unto you, that likewise joy shall be in heaven over one sinner
that repenteth, more than over ninety and nine just persons,
which need no repentance.

—Luke 15:3-7

CHAPTER 16

The Final Appointment

When God first led me to write this book, I sensed an urgency to complete it. After writing for well over a year, I was confident that I was approaching the finish line. Then, quite suddenly, my life took a devastating turn.

I learned that my mother was in a fight for her life and I knew she was unprepared for her most important appointment – her final appointment to stand before God. Many of her beliefs about her relationship with God and the fate of her soul were based on Christian fables. Some she embraced because that is what she had been taught. Others she embraced because they made her comfortable with sin.

As I cared for my mother in the final days of her life, I had to face a painful truth. My book was not written solely for the purpose of leading people I might never meet to salvation. God gave me this book as the battle plan for one of the toughest battles of my own life. The battle to save my mother's soul could not have been won without the knowledge I gained from the painstaking study God used to prepare me to write this book.

It was only after my mother's death, however, that I began to understand God's greater plan for the book. When I finally returned to writing,

I understood that He was calling me to share more than just biblical truths about salvation. He was also calling me to share how He led my mother, step by step, from sin to salvation. It is a painful story for me to write, but I must share it because it is much more than just a story about my mother. It is a deeply moving testimony of God's tenderness and His faithfulness to deliver miracle after miracle to find and save one lost sheep.

God meticulously orchestrated every detail of the final days of my mother's life to ensure that she was fully prepared for heaven. He also did it to validate His biblical truths – for *me*. Watching the miracles God performed in the last days of my mother's life established in me an unshakeable faith in His Word and His true plan of salvation.

Many people are living life unaware that they are running out of time. Running out of time to repent. Running out of time to accept God's final offer of salvation. My mother did not know that she was running out of time, but God knew. I am so thankful that He loved her enough to give her the time she needed to hear, believe, and obey the true Gospel of Jesus Christ.

It is my sincere prayer that my mother's story will strengthen and encourage others to choose salvation. More importantly, I pray that it will encourage those in the kingdom of God to fight to very end to lead others to salvation. We never know how God will use our words, actions, and prayers to help save another precious soul who is running out of time.

CHAPTER 17

The Faith To Move
A Mountain

The year was winding down and, as usual, I was beginning to prepare for the holidays. Nothing special. No travel plans. Just a quiet Thanksgiving and Christmas at home with my children.

Then, not long after Thanksgiving, God spoke to me and all my plans suddenly changed. The Lord told me to drop everything and go home to spend Christmas with my mother. I was puzzled. It was such short notice and Christmas that year was not a convenient time for me to travel. It seemed to me that there were so many more pressing concerns that needed my attention, but God said that I absolutely must go.

I wondered why I could not go the following year when I would have had more time to prepare. I was tempted to wait, but I sensed a great urgency, so I dropped everything and rearranged my plans. Although it was difficult to take time away from work and I didn't have the money in my budget, I went anyway. In the end, I was glad that I did. It turned out to be the perfect Christmas surprise arranged with the help of my oldest brother.

My children and I arrived a few days before Christmas and quietly slipped into my mother's house. My oldest brother, who had been visiting with her that day, called for her to come downstairs. He claimed that he needed her help finding something he had misplaced.

When my mother walked into the kitchen to help him, she discovered my children and me standing there to greet her. She could not have been more delighted. It was the best Christmas present I could have given her. I was so grateful that I rearranged my holiday plans and obeyed God.

My mother and I had a wonderful time celebrating the Christmas season together. We enjoyed our customary shopping spree and the pre-Christmas dinner my youngest brother and his wife hosted to celebrate my niece's birthday. A few days later, my mom and I cooked Christmas dinner together. Everything was absolutely perfect until the day after Christmas.

My mother woke up tired, not feeling much like getting out of bed. She seemed to be coming down with a cold. I thought perhaps the holidays had taken a bit of a toll on her, so I anointed her head with oil, prayed for her, and left her to rest in bed for the remainder of the day.

The following day she showed no signs of improvement, so I left her to rest for another day. The third day – not much change. She stayed in bed for the remainder of the week. Finally, it was time for me to leave. I hugged and kissed her and said my goodbyes, never doubting that soon she would be back to normal. I left looking forward to our next visit.

My mother was such a vibrant woman that most people were shocked when they learned her age. She loved life and her mind was a sharp as ever. Even her grandchildren were amazed that she stayed abreast of current events in every arena including pop culture. She was an avid sports fan who could still remember statistics for nearly every sport, professional and collegiate, for the last forty years.

She had such a zest for life. It seemed that she had so much more living to do. My brothers and I often joked that she would probably live longer than all of us. We all believed that she, like many women in her family, would probably live to be a hundred.

After returning home, I was surprised that each time I called my mother to check on her, she still showed no signs of improvement. Finally, in mid

January, God spoke to me again. He said that I would soon face a mountain, but that I should not worry. He explained that He had been preparing me for it for a long time and assured me that I would have enough faith to move the mountain.

I had no idea what He meant. All I knew was that I had a sick feeling in the pit of my stomach. I knew the mountain would soon surface, but it never occurred to me that it had anything to do with my mother.

A few days later, I got the call. My mother left me a message. She said she had been to the doctor, the test results were back, and the news was not good. When I returned her call, she shared with me that she had been diagnosed with lung cancer.

I was stunned, but I was not afraid. I knew that was the mountain God had warned me to expect. I also knew that He had already told me that I had faith enough to move it. It did not feel like I had enough faith to move that particular mountain, but I trusted God. My mother had been diagnosed with cancer a few years earlier. It was successfully treated, so I put my whole heart into believing that God would heal her again.

Over the next couple of months, my mother and I spoke almost daily. Each time we spoke, the news got progressively worse. The tumors were growing rapidly, her breathing was becoming more labored, and the pain was excruciating. The cancer was not responding to the medication. Her body was deteriorating and she needed a more aggressive plan of treatment.

I wanted to go home to see her, but I did not. Despite the devastating reports, I had a great sense of peace because of what God had said. I knew that it was not yet time for me to go and I trusted that God had the perfect plan. I trusted that just as He had spoken so clearly to me when He told me that I needed to go home for Christmas, He would speak again when it was time for me to return. So, I waited.

While I waited for God to speak, I listened to reports from my brothers about my mother's deteriorating health. She was having difficulty with mobility. A lift had to be installed in her home to transport her up and down the stairs. She could no longer walk from the car to her medical appointments. She needed a wheelchair. A live-in caregiver had been hired to cook and clean because she could no longer do those things for herself.

My mother and my brothers were gravely concerned. I heard it in all of their voices. Still, God did not send me home, so I continued to wait. For nearly three months, a dear friend and I labored tirelessly in prayer.

My friend's sister was in desperate need of a bone marrow transplant. For two months she had been bed ridden, deteriorating with no signs of improvement. She had a willing donor, but her doctors would not proceed with the surgery. The doctors had determined that she was too weak to travel out of state to the hospital where the surgery would be performed. More importantly, she was far too weak to undergo a transplant.

Cancer was savagely destroying the lives of my mother and my friend's sister. It seemed all but certain that both women soon would be gone. Nonetheless, my friend and I expected God to deliver miracles, so we continued daily in fervent prayer. We rose early each morning to pray and cry out to God for their healing.

Finally, on my mother's birthday, God spoke. He gave me a clear message to deliver to my mother. He also gave me a separate, but equally clear message to deliver to my friend's sister. When I heard what God had said concerning both women, I was ecstatic.

God told me to call my friend immediately and tell her to inform her sister that she would surely live. Not maybe, but *surely*. The report of her doctors did not matter. The condition of her body did not matter. How she felt did not matter. What she believed did not matter. God said that He was going to heal her and it was a finished work.

I tried all day to contact my friend. When I finally reached her to deliver the message God had given me, I learned that she also had news for me. She had spoken with her sister prior to speaking with me. I discovered that within hours after God spoke His promise, her sister's body was suddenly and miraculously strengthened. That night, after having been confined to her bed for two months, she got up and got dressed. For the first time in months, she left her home and went to church.

When her pastor received the call that she was on her way to church that evening, he was elated to hear about the sudden change in her condition. He was so delighted to have her back in church that he gave instructions to have her park in his space. She was in church that evening and the following day she was out walking and shopping with her husband.

It was a miracle and everyone knew it. God said it and before I could reach my friend to deliver the message, He had already begun to prove His Word. My friend was shocked when she heard what God had said to me. I was shocked when I heard what He had done for her sister within a matter of hours.

For three months we had been crying out to God, believing against all odds that He would heal our loved ones. That day, when I saw what He did for my friend's sister, I was certain that He would honor His promise to heal my mother. Finally, God had convinced me that I really did have the faith to move that mountain.

After rejoicing over the victory that God had given to my friend's sister, I was ready to call my mother to deliver His promise to her. It was not quite the same promise that He had made to my friend's sister, but it was a good enough promise for me.

God gave my friend's sister an unconditional promise that He would surely heal her. My mother's promise, on the other hand, was conditional upon her obedience. God impressed upon my heart that if my mother would do two things, she would live. He gave me the message to deliver to her, then He said that it was time for me to return home to see her.

CHAPTER 18

A Miraculous Healing

My mother and I dearly loved each other. There was nothing she would not have done for me and there was nothing that I would not have done for her. There was, however, one thing that had been a barrier between us for many years and I knew it would be an issue when I arrived at her home. That issue was religion.

For years, my mother had accused me of being too pushy about my religious beliefs. She was right. For years, I had accused her of being resistant to God and to the truth. I, too, was right, so religion remained a sore subject between us.

I continued to talk to her about God and attempt to delicately address the issue of one particular sin in her life. She continued to remind me that I needed to live my own life and mind my own business.

Occasionally she would remind me of my past sins. I tried to help her understand that, in God's eyes, there was a great difference between my sin and hers. The difference was that I had repented and she had not. Those sins were in my past. Her sin was still a part of her life. At the end of our conversations, she would typically remind me that she was free to make her own life choices just as I was free to make mine.

My mother failed to recognize that the fate of her soul was my business. She was my mother, she was my friend, and I loved her dearly. I loved her enough to be more concerned about her soul than I was about the possibility of offending her with the truth.

As I prepared to call my mother to deliver the message, I already knew that she would not want to hear what I had to say. I also knew that she would not want to do either of the two things God required of her. It never occurred to me, however, that she would die. My mother was standing face to face with death, so I was absolutely certain that she surely would do whatever was necessary to live.

When we finally spoke, I shared with my mother that God was sending me home to baptize her in the name of Jesus Christ. I also explained that He had instructed me not to leave until her baptism was complete. The second thing I shared with her was that before she could be baptized, she would have to repent and turn away from the sin that had stood between her and God for so many years. I told her that God said if she would do those two things, He would heal her and she would live.

My mother listened quietly. She had little to say when I finished. She knew that I was determined and she was absolutely right. I left little room for debate. She was my mother and one of my closest friends. I desperately needed her to live. I had already seen what God had done for my friend's sister, so I had no doubt that He would do the same for my mother.

After speaking with my mother, I began preparing for my trip. I bought my plane ticket, then I called one of my brothers to let him know that I was coming home. He was angry when I called because he felt that I should have come much sooner. He wanted to know what had taken me so long to decide to come home to see about our mother. I understood how he felt. However, all I told him was that I was coming home to see her and that she would improve.

My brother was understandably disturbed that I would suggest something that sounded so ridiculous. As far as he was concerned, I had lost my grip on reality. He had been there listening to the doctor's reports and watching our mother wither away. My promise of a miraculous healing for our mother was more than he was prepared to hear.

I certainly understood how my brother felt, but I also knew what God had said. God promised me a miracle and I fully expected to receive it. He told me that I had the faith to move that mountain and I intended to move it. That was all that mattered to me because my mother's life depended on that mountain being moved.

I called my pastor shortly before I was to visit my mother to make certain that I knew exactly how to baptize her. He gave me specific instructions, then he warned me not to try to baptize her in a bathtub. He insisted that I would not be able to fully immerse her in the water.

I had my assignment from God and my instructions from my pastor and that was all I needed. I boarded my flight and went home to baptize my mother.

My brother picked me up from the airport and we drove to my mother's home. When we arrived in her driveway, God stopped me just before I went into the house. He said I needed to brace myself because I was not prepared for what I was about to see.

When I walked into the house, I realized that I truly was not prepared. That night I found my mother lying in bed, moaning and writhing in pain. There was nothing but anguish in her once vibrant eyes. Her face was disfigured by uncontrollable grimaces and constant contortions from the pain. She could barely speak. Her breathing was agonizingly labored. My precious mother seemed as close to the brink of death as I could have imagined. Each time she gasped for air that night, I felt that breath might be her last.

If God had not spoken to me before I arrived, my heart would have been gripped with fear. Yet, He had made me a promise and I clung to it all night. That promise was the only hope I had. It was all that kept me believing that my mother would live to see the sun rise again.

As I lay in bed beside my mother watching her suffer, I wondered how I could ever accomplish what God had sent me to do. Baptizing her seemed like an impossible task, but I knew that I had to try. That night I began to talk to my mother, reminding her of the reason I had come. I reminded her of all that God had said.

She did not want to hear it before she became ill and she certainly did not want to hear it in the midst of the pain. All she could think about was fighting for her next breath, but all I could think about was fighting for her soul, so I continued to talk to her.

I explained to her about the importance of being baptized. She told me that she had already been baptized as a child when someone sprinkled water on her head. She insisted that God would accept that. Each time she told me what she was unwilling to do, I shared with her what the Bible says about that particular point. I shared that we cannot offer God what we choose to give Him and expect Him to accept it. We must learn what He requires of us and meet His requirements.

All the time we argued, I thought, "Father, you see that my mother can barely walk or breathe. How do You expect me to get her out of this house and to a place where I can baptize her?" I could not see how it would all come together. All I knew was that I was on an assignment and I was not leaving until I finished what God sent me to do.

My mother and I continued to talk until she finally began to surrender. She agreed that she would get baptized just to make me happy. I told her that she did not need to make me happy. She needed to repent for her sins and get baptized in the name of Jesus Christ so God could save her soul.

I knew that getting into the water was not the real problem my mother had to overcome. If she thought getting into a pool of water would have saved her, she would have gladly done it. The real problem was the sin. My mother did not want to let go of her sin, even though she knew that was exactly what she needed to do. She understood that without sincere repentance, baptism was pointless.

Finally, she quietly surrendered her heart to God and agreed to repent and be baptized. Not for me, but for herself, and for God.

Within one day after my mother surrendered her heart, God did what He promised that He would do. He miraculously strengthened her. The next day she was prescribed a new medication that eased her pain. Suddenly, that night, my mother was herself again.

That night my mother and I slept together in her bed and visited just like old times. We ate chocolate pudding in bed and talked until the wee hours of the morning. Usually I did most of the talking. That night she did all the talking and I just listened. She talked about old times, telling me stories from her childhood. She laughed so hard that she almost cried. We had the time of our lives. I have no idea how long she talked because she talked me to sleep.

In one day my mother was her old self again. Did the change in medication help? Without question, it helped. However, the change I witnessed within twenty-four hours did not come from a change in pain medication. It came from a change of heart that moved the hand of God on her behalf.

When I called my brothers the following day to share what had happened, they could hardly believe it. They had to come see for themselves. My brothers arrived later that day to find our mother just as I had reported.

She was out of bed in her favorite seat watching television in her sitting room. She was moving freely about her home, talking, laughing, and enjoying the company of her children and her dogs.

God said He would do it and He delivered on His promise. My heart was so encouraged. For the next several days, I enjoyed my mother's company and rejoiced in seeing what God was doing for her.

Periodically, I would gently prod her about when she might be ready to be baptized. She promised me that she would do it, but she said that she needed some time to decide when she would be ready. I knew that she needed time to deal with the issues of her heart, so I left her alone.

When she finally decided that she was ready to be baptized, she was still weak. I doubted that she was strong enough to get to a church and into a baptismal pool, so I devised my own plan. I decided to attempt to baptize her in her oversized Roman bathtub.

Her strength had increased, but she was still weak, so I helped her get out of bed and into the bathroom. I ran the water and got her into the tub, but from the very beginning it was a disaster. The water was too cold. The tub was too shallow. There was no way to fully immerse her in the water.

My pastor was absolutely right. I never should have attempted to baptize her in the bathtub. After all that effort to get her to agree to be baptized, I had failed. I had to explain to my mother that she had not been properly baptized and that we would have to find another location.

She was furious. She demanded that I baptize her right then. I told her that I simply could not. It was impossible for me to fully immerse her in that bathtub.

Still, she was determined that she was going to be baptized that night. She said that if I would not baptize her, she would do it herself. She pinched her nose closed, dipped her face in the water, and insisted that she was officially baptized in the name of Jesus Christ. As far as she was concerned, it was over. She said that she had done all she could do and that God would simply have to honor her efforts.

I told her that we would have to try again elsewhere. She was bitterly angry with me. She insisted that she could forgive me for many things, but this one thing was something she would never forgive or forget. She rightly accused me of ruining her baptism and she informed me that we were finished discussing the matter.

I was devastated. I had gotten so close, then botched my mother's baptism because I ignored my pastor's instructions. I knew that my mother would be in trouble if she rejected baptism and I would certainly be in trouble with God for failing to accomplish what He sent me to do. I had no idea how to recover. It seemed that I would never get my mother to the water again.

I helped her out of the tub, got her dried off, and back into bed. For the remainder of the night, I kept my mouth shut, prayed, and waited for God to speak again. I had made a mess and I desperately needed His help.

The next day I began calling a long list of churches to see if I could find one that would baptize my mother. There was no answer at most of the churches. I was so excited when I finally reached a pastor who was willing to baptize her. Then I discovered that his church had no baptismal pool.

The pastor indicated that he performs all of his baptisms at a nearby creek. That was where he proposed to baptize my mother. It seemed that I was fighting a losing battle. I knew there was no way to get my mother to a creek and, even if I could have gotten her there, I surely could not have convinced her to get into that cold water.

Finally, I sensed God leading me in a different direction, so I began to look for a country club with a heated swimming pool. Almost immediately after I began making calls, I found the perfect place. It was a private country club with a heated, indoor pool. When I asked if they had a wheelchair, God had a surprise for me. Not only did they have a wheelchair, it was a floating wheelchair that I could take into the pool. Best of all, the country club was located in the gated community where one of my brothers lives. Thankfully, that meant that I would have no difficulty gaining access to the facility.

Once again, I was absolutely in awe of God. I was so grateful to Him for providing a place for me to baptize my mother. I was even more grateful that He had softened her heart. My mother had settled down from the previous night's disaster and agreed to give me a second chance.

When my brother arrived to drive us to the country club, I knew he believed that I had coerced our mother into doing something she really did not want to do. He was certain that she was getting baptized simply to quiet my mouth. I knew otherwise. On the way to her baptism, my mother finally acknowledged that if baptism was required for her to get into heaven, she was willing to do it. That was her reason for agreeing to be baptized.

When we arrived at the country club, my brother got the wheelchair for her and pushed her inside. I helped her into the dressing room, got her changed into a swimsuit, then wheeled her to the pool.

My mother could not swim and she had always been afraid of water, so I explained to her what was about to happen. I reassured her that everything would be fine, then I wheeled her into the pool and baptized her in the name of Jesus Christ for the remission of her sins.

My brother stood on the edge of the pool silently watching. He said nothing, but I knew that he was upset. He did not understand what I was doing or why I was doing it. In his eyes, I had taken our sick mother who was afraid of the water into a swimming pool for a religious ritual that made me happy. I simply prayed that one day God would open his eyes to the truth.

When our mother came out of the water, I did not care what anyone other than Jesus thought in that moment. I knew what God had sent me to do. My job was done and I was grateful.

My mother was relieved as well, but she was also very weary. She had done what I told her God required of her. However, not long after her baptism was over, she insisted that from then on, she did not want to hear any more from me about God or religion. I agreed to leave her alone.

That evening I was excited to report the good news of my mother's baptism to my eighteen year old daughter. When I did, my daughter reminded me that her grandmother had not done all that was required to establish her salvation.

My mother still had not received the baptism of the Spirit. My daughter reminded me that I would need to return to finish that work with my mother.

I knew that my daughter was right, but I felt like she had just thrown a cold bucket of water in my face. She had no idea what I had been through just to get her grandmother baptized. The thought of explaining the rest of God's plan of salvation to my mother was more than I was prepared to handle in that moment. I knew that it was not yet time for that discussion, so I decided to enjoy the remaining time with my mother and leave that topic for another visit.

I stayed with my mother for two weeks on that particular visit. During that time, she went from the brink of death to being baptized in the name of Jesus Christ and having a renewed hope for life. By the time I returned home, God had supernaturally strengthened her body and she continued to gain strength daily.

My mother was sleeping comfortably through the night by the time I returned home. She cooked breakfast for me one morning before I left and had returned to her favorite morning ritual of cooking bacon for her two well-pampered little dogs. She had discontinued the services of her live-in caregiver and resumed her normal routine of light cooking and doing her own laundry. She no longer required the use of her lift to get up and down the stairs in her home. Instead of being pushed in a wheelchair, she was walking to and from the car to her medical appointments.

I witnessed God do all of that for my mother during the two weeks that I was with her. She was showing significant signs of improvement and she was returning to a life of independent living.

My mother certainly was not healed of cancer, but there was no doubt in my mind that God was beginning to restore her body and heal her. I had no doubt that He would continue to heal her if she would leave one particular sin in her past. That was the final warning I gave her before I returned home.

As long as I was there with her, I knew that she was fine. However, I knew that her true test would come when I was gone and she was forced to make tough choices on her own.

CHAPTER 19

A Long Journey Home

Not long after I returned home, I was disheartened to learn that my mother had not chosen wisely. She had disregarded what God said and made the wrong choice. She returned to the same sin that had stood between her and God for so long.

Not surprisingly, each time we spoke, she shared with me that her health was worsening. She was growing weaker. She was able to do less and less each day. I continued to pray for her and I believed with everything in my heart that God would strengthen her again and heal her. Sadly, I never heard that sound of strength return to her voice.

A few months later, God showed me a vision of my mother. In the vision, I could see how much her body and soul had deteriorated. She had allowed her heart to return to the same hardened state toward God that she had prior to her baptism.

God showed me that He would soon send me home to care for my mother and to deliver her from her suffering once again. This time, He promised me that my mother would not die, but that she would surely live. That promise was such a great comfort to me and it kept my heart at peace.

Soon after God spoke to me, I told my daughter that she needed to be prepared for me to leave again for an extended stay with her grandmother. I had no idea how soon God would send me, but I knew it would be soon.

A few days later, I received a call from one of my brothers. My mother had collapsed on her bedroom floor during the night. She was too weak to get up and had remained there all night. The following morning a visitor who stopped by to check on her found her lying on the floor of her bedroom. An ambulance was called and she was rushed to the hospital.

My mother remained hospitalized for quite some time. I decided to wait until she was released before going home to care for her. When I arrived at her home and saw her condition, I was deeply shaken. Her health had deteriorated more than I could have imagined. Her legs were so weak that she could no longer stand or walk. She could barely use her arms. She was confined to a hospital bed in her living room and she needed oxygen round the clock. The living room was filled with medical supplies and spare oxygen tanks. It looked to me as if my mother had been warehoused in a room just so she could die.

I could not bear the sight of her in that condition. I needed her to smile and laugh again. I needed her to eat chocolate pudding with me and tell me stories again. I needed her to walk and travel with me again.

For years, my mother had been my travel buddy. I needed her to get out of that bed and take just one more trip with me. Just one more trip was all I wanted.

As I looked at her in that bed, I knew that we had a monumental battle ahead of us. I was certain that I knew exactly what to do to make her better and I intended to do it. I believed with all my heart that if I just got busy doing what I do best, God would keep His promise and fix everything.

My mother had three wonderful sons who are also wonderful brothers to me. I was her only daughter. My brothers always did the things for her that daughters don't typically do. They fixed things in her home and took her to football games to see her favorite team. They bought her electronic gadgets and programmed them so all she had to do was push the buttons.

Those were not the things I did for her. I knew how to make things beautiful for my mother and I knew how to pray for her. I was certain that if I could just do those two things with all my heart, she would get better. So, I got busy working on making her live.

I asked one of my brothers to move the oxygen tanks into the garage. I wanted them neatly tucked away where they did not constantly remind me that she needed oxygen tanks to help her breathe. The sight of them made me think that she just might die.

I put pretty linen on her hospital bed and got rid of those sterile white sheets. That torn white t-shirt she was wearing had to go. I wanted her dressed in the pretty pajamas that she so loved, so I changed her clothes. No one had combed her hair since she had come home from the hospital, so I shampooed and combed it.

The living room furniture had not been properly rearranged after the hospital bed and medical equipment were delivered. I got busy rearranging the furniture, cleaning the room, and buying fresh flowers for the coffee table. Pretty things always made my mother feel better, so I worked on making things beautiful while God healed her.

Her dogs were next on the list. My mother always kept them well groomed, but they were dirty, so I cleaned them, too. I wanted them bathed and neatly groomed so they could get on her bed and visit with her. She loved those little dogs and I was certain that spending time with them would help her recover.

I believed that if I just worked and prayed hard enough, God would heal her for me. He was my only God and she was my only mother. I desperately needed both of them. God knew that. I had to believe that He loved me too much to let my mother die, so I did my best to do my part. Round the clock, I worked and prayed, but she didn't get better.

One day I finally realized that she could no longer drink from a cup, nor could she sip from a straw. She was too weak to suck. I wanted to believe that somehow I could fix that for her, so I ran out to the store and bought colorful baby bottles. I cut holes in the nipples and fed her from a bottle. I laughed while I fed her, telling her that it wasn't really a baby bottle. It was a sports bottle and she was training like an athlete. She knew better, but she smiled anyway just to humor me.

All the while everyone around me knew that my mother was dying, but I truly did not know. I was still holding onto God's second promise to me that my mother would live. That is what I told my brothers. I told them that God had promised that she would live and I believed Him.

I even read them the Scripture God gave me about Lazarus being resurrected from the dead. I promised them that God would resurrect our mother just as He resurrected Lazarus.

My brothers looked at me as if I had lost my mind, but I did not care. Against all odds, I trusted and believed in my promise from God. All the while that I trusted God for a miracle, my mother inched closer and closer to death.

Eventually, I knew I had prayed all that I could. I knew that I had to talk to my mother about God again. I tried talking to her, encouraging her to pray. Pray again. Pray harder.

Finally, my mother reminded me that she had already told me on my last visit that she did not want to hear anything else from me about God. She said that she had prayed until she could pray no more. It seemed that there was nothing left for me to do but trust God for another miracle. And, indeed, God delivered that miracle.

Soon thereafter, the hospice nurse came to visit one Thursday afternoon. According to the nurse, we had run out of time. She assured us that our mother would be dead within a matter of hours. She handed us a prescription and suggested that we fill it immediately.

The prescription was for medication to ease the pain and put my mother to sleep. The nurse suggested that we say our final goodbyes to our mother before giving her the medication. She advised us that once we gave her the medication, she would likely never awaken. Before leaving, the nurse closed out my mother's file. She said her goodbyes to us and informed us that she did not expect to return for another visit.

Just before she left, she gave us instructions regarding who to contact to have our mother's body removed from the home that evening. I heard everything the nurse said, but I did not believe for one minute that my mother would die. Over that weekend, God supernaturally strengthened her body once again.

When the following week arrived, the hospice nurse returned for her scheduled visit. Much to her surprise, not only was my mother not dead, she was quite determined to live. My mother was a fighter and she was fighting for her life. She wanted to walk again and she wanted to go outside again. That was her goal. She wanted to get strong enough to get into a wheelchair and sit outside in the sunshine on her patio.

When the nurse saw what God had done for my mother, she agreed to order physical therapy treatments for her. I was so excited. I believed with all my heart that I had finally witnessed the miracle that God had so faithfully promised me. I was certain that my mother was on the road to recovery and I knew it was time for her to receive the baptism of the Spirit. God had shown me in a dream a few days earlier that He would soon fill my mother with His Spirit. He also showed me in that dream that as soon as she received His Spirit, He was going to take her home to be with Him.

I clearly heard what He said, but my heart was only prepared to believe half of it. I knew it was time for my mother to receive God's Spirit. Still, I refused to believe that He would take her from me, so I held onto the promise that she would live.

When God miraculously strengthened her body, I began to hope again. I sat beside her bed and began talking with her about God just one more time. As I spoke, I could see that God had softened her heart. She listened intently as I told her about what it means to be filled with God's Spirit. I shared with her that whether she lived or died, she would need to receive the baptism of the Spirit.

I explained that if she lived, she would need God's Spirit to intercede on her behalf and help her through the healing process. And, if she died, she would need to be filled with His Spirit to make it into heaven. I explained that either way, she could not live or die without receiving God's Spirit.

She listened quietly and I knew that the truth was beginning to work its way into her heart. However, it wasn't until I shared with her how close she had come to death that my words really began to register in her spirit.

My mother had no idea that the nurse had believed that she was only hours away from death. When I shared with her how close she had come to death, my mother was stunned. In that moment of sobering truth, I saw the fear of God grip her heart. From that moment on, she held onto every word I spoke.

One of my brothers came into the room as we were talking. He knew that we were likely talking about God. He also knew there was a chance that our mother would not want to hear what I had to say. He asked her if she wanted to continue the conversation with me, so I quietly waited for her answer.

My mother could barely speak, but she let my brother know that this time she wanted to hear. I was so thankful that God had touched her heart. My brother left the room and my mother and I continued our conversation. I told her that I would pray with her to receive the baptism of the Spirit.

I helped her to raise her arms and I told her to open her mouth and praise and glorify God. I promised her that God would fill her with His Spirit if she asked Him from a sincere, repentant heart.

When my mother surrendered her heart to God, He filled her with His Spirit and gave her the precious gift of the Holy Ghost, just as He promised. I was so thankful for what God did for my mother and I was still hopeful. As sick as she was, I still did not believe that she would die.

I had been with my mother on that particular visit for nearly a month caring for her day and night. I was exhausted. I finally decided that it was time for me to return to my home for a brief visit. I needed to check on my daughter and settle some personal affairs at my home.

My brothers agreed to care for our mother while I was gone. I told them that I would book a flight home that week and return soon thereafter to continue caring for her.

However, just as I was about to book my flight, my mother took a turn for the worse. I knew that I could not leave her. I had to wait for God to strengthen her again before I returned home, so I stayed and continued to care for her and pray for her.

She got worse by the hour. I prayed harder. I called friends and my pastors to ask them to pray for her. I cried out to God with all my heart, pleading with Him in desperation to do what He had promised. Still, she drew closer to death.

I had never seen my mother weaker. I was absolutely despondent and desperate for just one more miracle. I needed God to do something – anything – to help her and to help me.

Later that morning, my phone rang. It was a call from someone I had not spoken with in months. I had no intention of taking the call at that moment as I sat with my mother, but I sensed God prompting me to answer the phone. I could not understand why.

When I finally answered the phone, I said nothing about my mother. I just greeted the woman and listened to what she had to say. She shared with me that she was sitting at a bus stop waiting for a bus to take her to a nursing home. She decided to call me to chat while she waited. She said that she was going to pray with the sick and elderly and sing to them. When I inquired about why she planned to sing to them, she explained that singing seemed to comfort them. It was such a strange thing to me. We only spoke for a few minutes, and then she had to go.

When we got off the phone, the Lord spoke to me again. He said that was what He wanted me to do. He wanted me to sing to my mother that day. So, I cuddled with her. I held her hand, stroked her hair, and softly sang gospel songs in her ear.

I talked to my mother and whispered things to her that she needed to hear. That was the day that I stopped encouraging her to fight to live. I finally told her that it was all right for her to die.

I knew that she was worried about me. She worried about whether I would be all right without her. I assured her that I would be fine and that God will always take care of me just as He had always taken care of her. I reminded her that she had taught me everything I need to know to finish my race and I promised her that I will finish strong. I gently whispered in her ear everything she needed to hear so she could die in peace.

That day I gave up my fight for my mother so she could give up fighting to live for me. I finally realized that I had to let her go. The only remaining hope God had given her was the hope of eternal life. I knew that my only hope of seeing her again will be when I walk through the gates of heaven and I finally had to accept that.

When I finally let my mother go, I promised her that Jesus was coming for her to take her home. Then I sang sweetly to her and I encouraged her to hold onto every ounce of her faith until He came.

As I snuggled close to my mother on that bed for the last time, I was reminded of something that had always been a joke between us. My mother and I had always laughed about her sense of smell. She had a pretty little nose and it seemed as if that nose of hers could smell the slightest odor a mile away. If there was one thing my mother hated, it was a foul smell. She would leave any room at even the hint of an unpleasant odor.

My mother loved sweet smelling things and she loved to smell sweet. She began collecting perfume before I was born. That forever sweet aroma was one of my earliest childhood memories of my mother and it was one of my daughter's earliest memories of her, too. Even as a little, girl my daughter always told me how much she loved to hug her grandmother and savor that sweetness.

That day as I lay next to my mother, there was a different smell that filled the air. It was the smell of death. It had been lingering in that room for weeks. No one ever mentioned it to my mother, but she knew it was there. She mentioned it to me one day as she neared the end of her life.

I knew how much she hated that odor, but this time she could not leave the room. She couldn't walk away from that smell and I couldn't walk away from her. So in our final days together, that awful smell was our constant, unwelcome companion as she lay dying in that bed.

The day my mother died, I knew there was little I could do to make life beautiful for her again. The only thing I could think to do was give her one last little bit of something she loved. I went upstairs to her bedroom and got her favorite perfume.

Every time I smelled that perfume as a little girl, I knew that she and my father were going out for a special occasion. Before leaving, she would always bend down to kiss me goodbye. After the kiss, I would pull her close to me one more time so I could savor the smell.

I put some of my mother's favorite perfume on her just before she died so she and I could enjoy that beautiful fragrance on her just one last time. I knew it was there, but I couldn't smell it and I doubt that she could. The smell in the room overpowered the perfume, but that didn't matter to me. My mother smiled when I whispered to her that I had put her favorite perfume on her. That was all that mattered.

I cuddled beside my mother that evening and pulled her close to me just one more time. She died as I held her hand, stroked her hair, and sang softly in her ear.

As hard as it was, I had to accept that God had kept His promise to me. He promised me that He would raise my mother from the dead and make her live again. He did just that, though not in the manner I had hoped He would. He brought her back from a spiritual death, gave her the gift of eternal life, and took her from this world before the devil could touch her perfected soul.

CHAPTER 20

Miriam's Song

When God seals our adoption and welcomes us into His kingdom, He washes away our past, gives us a brand new beginning, and receives us as holy and acceptable to Him. That is how my mother died. She was a brand new creation in Jesus Christ, covered with His precious blood and filled with His Spirit. That is how I will remember her. My mother was precious to me and she was unquestionably precious to God. I want to end by giving her the honor she deserves as my mother and my friend.

My mother's name was Miriam Arie Trotter McNeil. Her life was a gift to me. I loved her with all of my heart and soul. Yet, somehow, she always made me feel that no matter how much I loved her, she loved me more. She was an amazing woman, mother, and friend to me. For all that she was to me, I will be ever grateful.

More than anything, my mother's life was about love. She was the person who celebrated my successes when I was strong. She supported me in every way when I was weak. She provided for my children and me when I was too sick to care for us. She listened when I needed a friend. She believed in me when I lost confidence in myself. She encouraged me when I was certain that I could not go on.

My mom was everything that I could have asked for in a mother. She was more than I could have hoped for in a friend. She did much good in the lives of many. I am certain, however, that she gave more of her life for my children and me than she did for anyone else. I would not be the woman I am today without her.

From the very beginning, my mother's life was not was not easy. She was only nine months old when her mother died. When her father's work prevented him from being able to properly care for his two young children, he sent my mother and her older brother to another state to live with family. After learning of the abuse they were suffering at the hands of their caregivers, he arranged for them to be moved once again to live with other family members. Throughout my mother's early life she was cared for by various family members. She spent most of her formative years as a city girl in the country trying to survive in a place where she simply did not fit.

It was through my mother's stories that I became well acquainted with the great sorrows of a motherless child. Unlike my mother, I, like most children, took many things about having a mother for granted. My mother's face was almost always the first face that greeted me each morning when she came to my room to awaken me. Her voice was usually the first sound I heard. My name had a familiar ring when I heard it come from her lips. I could often tell what she wanted simply from the way she spoke my name. From the day I was born until the day she died, my mother was there for me.

My mother, on the other hand, became acquainted with her mother by listening to stories told by her grandmother and rummaging through an old chest in her grandmother's home that was filled with her mother's dresses. Family photographs were rare in the small, rural town where my mother resided, so there were no pictures of her mother in their home. My mother was a teen when she finally saw one of the few photographs ever taken of her mother. It was given to her as a gift by a family friend who learned that she had never seen a picture of her mother.

Sadly, my mother was also a teen before she learned her own real name. When she went to live with family members as a young child, her name was mispronounced and misspelled. Consequently, she went through life believing that her name was Myron. Eventually, my mother met someone who knew her parents in the state where they resided at the time she was born. That individual shared with my mother that her mother had, in fact, named her Miriam after Miriam in the Bible. Myron, however, remained her legal name throughout her life. I am the only person who ever acknowledged her as Miriam.

Soon after high school, she left country living far behind and moved west to join her father and brother. After a brief marriage that ended in divorce, she met and married my father. During their marriage, my father's career moved our family more than twenty times across the U.S. and abroad. Through all of our travels, my mother unselfishly gave great love and care to all who depended upon her. She provided stability, comfort, and security for a husband and four children. Without her, daily life for our closely knit family would not have been possible. Though my mother grew up without the love of her own mother, she was a wonderful mother to my brothers and me. She was an equally devoted wife.

However, nearly thirty years after marrying my father, their marriage ended in divorce, and all the odds were against her. In her early fifties, she was broke, alone, with little college, and no recent work experience.

My mother struggled initially, working odd jobs. Eventually, she secured an entry level civil service job. She began her career working in the basement as a mail clerk. For nearly twenty five years, my mother commuted over a hundred miles roundtrip each day. During that time, she went back to school to earn her degree. By the grace of God and through her own perseverance, she ended her career on top. She retired as a Branch Chief in a large federal agency with responsibility for operations in two major metropolitan areas.

My mother worked hard, built her savings, and invested wisely. In the end, she beat the odds. She retired quite comfortably and was able to provide well for herself and for many others in their times of need.

In her later years, my mother enjoyed leisure travel with my children and me. She enjoyed quality time with her own children, extended family, friends, and her dogs. She was also active in her community.

I often jokingly reminded my mother that she was a late bloomer who, against all odds, always managed to bloom beautifully. She began her career late in life, but she ran a strong race and finished at the top. She gave her life to Christ late in life. Securing her salvation was the toughest race of her life, but she ran it with excellence. She crossed the finish line in victory and she claimed her crown.

No one is perfect. My mother was no exception, but I am certain that she was absolutely the perfect mother for me. She was a woman who was fiercely determined to overcome any and every obstacle. She overcame every obstacle in this life. She overcame every obstacle that stood between her and eternal life. She was a woman of great elegance and grace who successfully navigated many challenges in life. She was a fighter and a survivor. Most importantly, she was one of God's sheep.

I am so thankful that God allowed me the privilege of running the final leg of her race with her. Today I understand that we ran it together for a purpose. I ran with my mother to cheer her on as she crossed the finish line in victory. I also ran with her so I could take the baton that she reached back to hand to me just before she crossed over.

The baton that my mother handed me is the amazing story of her journey to meet Jesus Christ. Deep repentance. Baptism in the name of Jesus Christ for the remission of her sins. The baptism of the Spirit. Faith. That is what got my mother the victory, and that is why I unapologetically tell the truth from the Word of God that will lead others to salvation.

My mother finished her race ready to cross the finish line and step right through heaven's gates. There, she will enjoy an eternal celebration of song and dance and sweet rest in the mansion Jesus prepared just for her.

Today when I think of my mother, I am reminded of another Miriam. Moses led the children of Israel through the raging waters of the Red sea, but it was his sister, Miriam, who led the women in a great victory celebration of song and dance. This is what Exodus 15:18-21 says occurred when the children of Israel arrived safely on the other side:

The Lord shall reign for ever and ever.

For the horse of Pharaoh went in with his chariots and with his horse-men into the sea, and the Lord brought again the waters of the sea upon them; but the children of Israel went on dry land in the midst of the sea.

And Miriam the prophetess, the sister of Aaron, took a timbrel in her hand; and all the women went out after her with timbrels and with dances.

And Miriam answered them, Sing ye to the Lord, for he hath triumphed gloriously; the horse and his rider hath he thrown into the sea.

What a celebration! My mother always loved to dance. I enjoy imagining her and the Miriam whose name she carried leading the celebration of the saints who make it through the water and arrive safely inside those beautiful gates. I imagine her celebrating her brand new life and making brand new friends. Most of all, I enjoy imagining her enjoying luxurious living in the brand new mansion Jesus prepared just for her.

I, on other hand, am just beginning the next leg of the race. It's time for me to take the baton she handed me so I can run hard to win souls for Christ. Every step of the way, I run with the full assurance that one day I will step through those beautiful gates and join my mother in that grand, never ending dance. Until we meet again, with the deepest gratitude, love, and admiration, I thank and salute my mother and my dear friend who also became my sister in Christ.

AUTHOR'S NOTE

The day God took my mother home, He was also faithfully working on behalf of my friend's sister who was in the hospital preparing to receive her transplant.

Almost immediately after God spoke His promise concerning her life and miraculously strengthened her body, He continued to strengthen her daily. The sudden changes in her life were remarkable. Almost immediately, every report from her doctors was better than expected. All of her test results moved in the right direction, she was cleared for travel, and her doctors authorized her to receive the bone marrow transplant. My friend became her sister's donor, and the bone marrow she donated was a perfect match. In less than ninety days after God released His Word, she was in the hospital preparing for her life-saving bone marrow transplant. The results of the surgery were near perfect, the healing process was accelerated, and she was released from the hospital before her estimated release date. She left the hospital as a walking miracle without a trace of cancer in her body.

She is a woman who witnessed the salvation of the Lord after one whisper from God changed the trajectory of her life in a single day. Her restored life is a testimony of God's goodness, His mercy, and His grace.

HOW TO CONNECT WITH OUR COMMUNITY

The Desperate Zone

The Desperate Zone is our Christ-centered Learning Community designed for people who are in passionate pursuit of the biblical truth that leads to extraordinary transformation in ministry and life. With separate learning paths for *People in the Pulpit* and *People in the Pews*, our Learning Center offers exceptional online courses and learning resources for each phase of your journey. Learn to practically apply God's Word, follow His Spirit, and birth His signs, wonders, and miracles like the first community of born again believers in Acts 2.

Visit **www.desperatezone.com** to learn more. Be sure to order the complete three-volume series of *The Salvation Conversation* if you haven't already done so. The series includes *Green Balloon Miracles: The Path to Living a Life of Miracles*, *Are You Really Saved? Common Christian Fables About Salvation*, and *God's Little Army: Salvation Made Simple for Children*.

Made in the USA
Middletown, DE
20 June 2021